D0153900

# Pocket
# Reference for
# WRITERS

# How to Use the Pocket Handbook

The *Pocket Reference for Writers,* Second Edition, has been carefully crafted to save you time when you need answers. Keep this handbook near you when you are writing. When you have a question, use the following tools to help you find what you need.

The detailed **Contents** (beginning on the inside front cover) lists the specific topics covered in each chapter.

The colored sections on the outer edge of the pages provide a quick reference to the various documentation styles: **MLA** (first), **APA** (second), **CM** (third).

The complete index in the back of the handbook lists, in alphabetical order, all the subjects covered in the book. The index is most useful when you know the name of the term for which you are searching.

The *Pocket Reference for Writers,* Second Edition, contains two glossaries placed before the index. They reference the following material:

> The **Glossary of Usage** explains the differences between commonly confused words.

> The **Glossary of Grammatical Terms** provides clear explanations of technical grammatical terms, from pronouns to present tense and past participle.

***Want interactive practice exercises?*** Visit the Web site ***www.prenhall.com/ipractice*** for interactive, self-graded exercises on grammar, style, and punctuation as well as useful Web links and additional online resources.

# Pocket Reference for WRITERS

### SECOND EDITION

## Toby Fulwiler
University of Vermont

### AND

## Alan R. Hayakawa
*The Patriot News*
Harrisburg, Pennsylvania

PEARSON

Prentice
Hall

Upper Saddle River, New Jersey 07458

Library of Congress Cataloging-in-Publication Data

Fulwiler, Toby (date)
  Pocket reference for writers / Toby Fulwiler and Alan R. Hayakawa—2nd ed.
    p. cm.
  Includes index.
  ISBN 0-13-185024-5
  1. English language—Rhetoric—Handbooks, manuals, etc. 2. English
language—Grammar—Handbooks, manuals, etc. 3. Report writing—
Handbooks, manuals, etc. I. Hayakawa, Alan R. II. Title.
  PE1408.F815 2004
  808'.042—dc22

                                                              2004040148

**Editorial Director: Leah Jewell**
**Senior Acquisitions Editor: Stacy Best Ruel**
**Editorial Assistant: Steven Kyritz**
**VP, Director of Production and Manufacturing: Barbara Kittle**
**Senior Production Editor: Shelly Kupperman**
**Senior Media Editor: Christy Schaack**
**Web/Media Production Manager: Lynn Pearlman**
**Executive Marketing Manager: Brandy Dawson**
**Marketing Manager: Emily Cleary**
**Marketing Assistant: Allison Peck**
**Manufacturing Manager: Nick Sklitsis**
**Prepress and Manufacturing Buyer: Mary Ann Gloriande**
**Interior and Cover Designer: Laura Gardner**
**Electronic Artist: Mirella Signoretti**
**Copyeditor: Bruce Emmer**
**Proofreader: Judy Kiviat**
**Composition: Pine Tree Composition**
**Printer/Binder: Quebecor World Book Services**
**Cover Printer: Coral Graphics**
**Cover Illustration: Steve Vidler/Superstock, Inc.**

**Pearson Prentice Hall™** is a trademark of Pearson Education, Inc.
**Pearson®** is a registered trademark of Pearson plc
**Prentice Hall®** is a registered trademark of Pearson Education, Inc.

Pearson Education LTD. London
Pearson Education Singapore, Pte. Ltd
Pearson Education, Canada, Ltd
Pearson Education–Japan
Pearson Education Australia PTY, Limited
Pearson Education North Asia Ltd
Pearson Educación de Mexico, S.A. de C.V.
Pearson Education Malaysia, Pte. Ltd
Pearson Education, Upper Saddle River, NJ

10 9 8 7 6 5
ISBN 0-13-185024-5

# A Writer's Questions

Every act of writing addresses three questions: (1) Why are you writing? (2) Who is your audience? and (3) What is your situation? How you answer these questions largely shapes the voice you project on paper. To help you figure out the **purpose, audience, situation,** and **voice** in any writing task, it helps to have a reliable writing process that works for you. This first set of chapters examines more closely each of these dimensions of composing college papers.

# 1    What Is the Purpose?

When you write a personal letter, you know why you are doing it and what you hope to accomplish. However, when you write in response to a school assignment, your instructor sets the purpose, and it becomes your job to figure it out. Regardless of who instigates it, thoughtful writing is purposeful writing. To succeed, you need to know why you are writing and what you hope to accomplish.

## 1a.    Writing to discover

Writing helps people think as well as record what they've already thought. Writing makes language, and therefore thought, visible and permanent, allowing writers to understand, critique, rearrange, and correct their ideas. Discovery writing is written primarily for the writer, not for a distant or judgmental audience. Consequently, style, structure, and correctness matter less in discovery writing than invention, exploration, and honesty. Forms of discovery writing include the following:

- *Freewriting*
- *Journal and diary writing*
- *Letters or e-mail to trusted people*
- *Personal notes and lists*
- *Early drafts of formal papers*

Although instructors sometimes ask to see samples of discovery writing, they seldom correct or evaluate it. Whether assigned or not, such informal writing will help you learn virtually any subject better. You are writing to discover when you think about how to approach assignments, find topics, locate research sources, or just find out what's on your mind. For more on discovery writing, see Chapters 6 through 10.

## 1b.    Writing to communicate

The general purpose of most writing in college and the world at large is to communicate to audiences other than the writer. More specific purposes include communicating with the intention of reporting, informing, persuading, and exploring. To communicate clearly, writing needs to be

- Clear, to be understood
- Conventional, to enhance understanding and minimize confusion
- Supported and documented, to create belief or bolster credibility.

You are writing to communicate when an assignment asks you to *explain, report, analyze, describe, discuss, compare, contrast, interpret, argue,* or *evaluate* to an audience other than yourself. The majority of this pocket handbook explains and illustrates the conventions and guidelines most appropriate for academic writing.

## 1c.    Writing to create

Creative writers pay special attention to form, shape, rhythm, imagery, and the symbolic qualities of language. The term *creative writing* is usually associated with poetry, fiction, and drama but should apply to any text written with care, craft, and originality. For example, researching slave conditions in 1850s Virginia and then writing a narrative from the point of view of an escaped slave can be a creative yet highly factual paper at the same time—interesting to write and interesting to read. Although creative writing is also a type of communicative writing, its focus is less on audience and more on the shape of the expression itself.

Only a few college assignments may ask you to write creative papers, but many more conventional papers will profit from imaginative approaches that increase reader interest. You are invited to write creatively when an assignment asks you to *suppose, speculate, design, imagine, create,* or *invent.*

## 2    Who Is the Audience?

Writing is good when it communicates clearly to its intended audience. To address readers effectively, it helps if you imagine what they already know and believe as well as what their questions might be. Note how differently you would write to a friend or to a college instructor. With your friend, you assume shared experiences and a common sense of humor, allowing you to be playful with both content and style. With your instructor, however, you can assume very little, which means you need to explain a lot—and very carefully.

Instructors are especially difficult audiences because (1) they know what they expect from their assignment, (2) they often know more about the subject of your paper than you do, and (3) each has a personally distinct set of expectations. However, all instructors expect papers to demonstrate *accurate knowledge, critical reasoning,* and *literate language skills.*

- **Knowledge.** A successful paper demonstrates what you know and how well you know it. If you argue for or against affirmative action policies, for example, you must demonstrate that you know about recent civil rights history and current political debates. A successful college paper has accurate facts, clear definitions, careful explanations, and up-to-date information.

- **Critical reasoning.** A successful paper reveals your ability to reason logically and consistently, to support assertions, to organize information, and to be persuasive. In arguing for or against tighter gun control laws, offer reasons for your position and refute opposing arguments. Critical reasoning is witnessed in the clarity and arrangement of your ideas, the justness of your claims, and the persuasiveness of your evidence.

- **Language skills.** Instructors notice the clarity and correctness of your language, especially when your sentences are not clear or your spelling, punctuation, or grammar is incorrect. You are expected to turn in papers that are neat, legible, and carefully edited according to standard academic conventions (see Chapters 53–66).

# 3 What Is the Situation?

When you write college papers, remember that you are in an academic community that may differ in important ways from a home, high school, or work community. This larger academic community has clear expectations for what your papers should do and how they should appear.

- **Truth.** Regardless of department or discipline, members of the university community are committed to the pursuit of truth. Each academic discipline pursues truth in a particular way—the sciences one way, the social sciences another, the humanities still another. A successful college paper demonstrates that its writer can use the knowledge and methods of the discipline in which it has been assigned to reveal something that is true.

- **Evidence.** Scholars in all disciplines use credible evidence to support the truths they claim. Scientists make claims about the physical world and cite evidence to support those claims; art historians make similar claims about creative expression, and so on. As a college writer, make claims, assertions, or arguments that you believe to be true; then support those with the best facts, examples, and illustrations available. Always document the sources for this evidence.

- **Balance.** It is difficult or even impossible to prove that something is absolutely true because new information constantly calls old conclusions into question. Consequently, academic writers make claims cautiously, using balanced, judicious language positioned somewhere between authority and doubt. Your own authority as a college writer will be based on how well you read, reason, and write. Academic convention suggests that you present your inferences, assertions, and arguments in neutral, serious, nonemotional language and be fair to opposing points of view.

# 4    Finding Your Voice

Writing voices range from assertive to tentative, loud to quiet, serious to sarcastic, clear to garbled, and so on. Each of us is capable of projecting one or more of these voices at one time or another. Some voices win people over and inspire trust and others do not—and you need to figure out which does which. An appropriate voice for a particular paper reflects the larger academic community in which you are writing as well as your own unique background and personal experience. Your purpose, audience, and situation go a long way toward determining that voice—and so does who you are and where you come from. Think about the *tone, style, structure,* and *bias* of the voice you present in your writing.

■ **Tone.** The attitude you adopt toward a subject and audience is reflected in your tone: passionate, indifferent, puzzled, friendly, annoyed, and so on. Tone is something you control in everyday speech when you speak gently to a baby, cautiously to a teacher, or sarcastically to your friends. On paper, you control tone by selecting and emphasizing words, sentence type, and punctuation to approximate the mood you want to project. To control tone, read out loud everything you write and ask, Does it sound as I intend? If not, rewrite until it does.

■ **Style.** Style includes your choice and use of words, the construction and length of sentences, and the way the grammar and mechanics present your ideas on the page. Style can be described as formal (careful in respect to both convention and assertion), informal (more casual in form and mechanics), or colloquial (which sounds like talk written down). Unless circumstances dictate otherwise, write college papers in a semiformal style that is clear, precise, and direct yet sounds like a real human being speaking—perhaps a style similar to that used in this handbook.

■ **Structure.** Structure concerns the organization of a whole paper and the relationships among the parts within the paper. The structure of a text suggests the thought process that created it. For example, writing with a logical structure suggests similar habits of mind, whereas writing with a circular or associative structure suggests more intuitive habits of mind. Some papers might call for a more logical self, others a more intuitive self; skillful writers could go either way. To control structure ask, How should the text open? Where should it go next? How should it conclude?

- **Bias.** When you write, you convey—directly or indirectly—what you believe socially, politically, culturally, and so on. Unless you deliberately mislead, your personal biases will be somewhere in the foreground or background of everything you write. Learn when personal values are expected (personal essays) and when they are not (lab reports). Examine drafts for opinion and judgment words that reveal your values, and keep or remove these words as appropriate.

## 5   Learning a Process

The process of writing academic papers from beginning to end can be complicated, frustrating, and exhilarating all at the same time. Good papers sometimes begin as vague notions, other times as specific intentions. For serious writers, rewriting is an essential part of the process as they re-examine their first thoughts, look for answers, fill in gaps, shore up arguments, and write new introductions—usually the last thing they write. Thoughtful papers conclude with careful editing and line-by-line proofreading to guarantee clarity and correctness. Most writers wish they could follow simple formulas to guarantee success, but there are no such formulas.

For discussion purposes, we can describe five distinct phases of writing in the approximate order in which they might occur: *planning, drafting, researching, revising,* and *editing*—although they may occur in any order and at many different times as you write.

Regardless of how you mix these phases, what matters is that you learn how this process works best for you and how practicing it helps you produce successful papers.

- **Planning.** Asking questions, trying out answers, and developing directions are all part of getting started. You are planning deliberately when you make notes, turn casual lists into organized outlines, write journal entries, compose rough drafts, and consult with others. You also plan less deliberately while you walk, jog, eat, read, and converse with friends or when you wake up in the middle of the night with an idea. Planning occurs, one way or another, every time you think about and try to solve a problem. (See Chapters 6–10 for specific planning strategies.)

- **Drafting.** At some point, all writers move beyond planning and actually start writing. Drafting happens when you try to advance your solution to a problem and see whether or not it works. The secret to productive writing is sitting down and beginning. A first draft is concerned with developing ideas, finding direction, clarifying concepts—in short, finding out what, exactly, the paper needs to say. Of course, you hope that your first draft will be final, but a rereading often suggests otherwise. (See Chapters 11–13 for drafting strategies.)

- **Researching.** College papers require precise information rather than vague knowledge. For such papers, active researching may take place prior to any drafting or while the writing is going on. The library and Internet provide new textual information, while interviews and site visits supply field data. Research also includes rereading textbooks, consulting dictionaries, conducting laboratory experiments, asking questions, and visiting museums. (See Chapters 47–51 for in-depth strategies for writing with research.)

- **Revising.** Somewhere in the middle to later stages of composing, writers begin revising the drafts they have planned, drafted, and researched. Revising involves rewriting to make the purpose clearer, the argument stronger, the details sharper, the evidence more convincing, the organization more logical. True revising is not just tinkering with words and punctuation but reseeing ideas and thinking again about direction, arguments, and evidence. (See Chapters 14 and 15 for revision strategies.)

■ **Editing.** Editing means sharpening, condensing, and clarifying the language. Editing is paying careful attention to specific words, striving for the most clarity and punch possible. Editing is rearranging sentences, finding strong verbs, and eliminating wordy constructions. The final stage of editing is proofreading—reading line by line with a ruler, correcting errors in spelling, typos, punctuation, and grammar. (See Chapters 16–46 for editing strategies.)

# Writing to Discover

For many writers, the most difficult part of writing is getting started. It is especially daunting to write a paper that will be evaluated for a grade, so it is easy to put off the writing until the night before it is due. However, trying to write both the first and the final draft at the last minute seldom results in either good learning or good writing. The following suggestions will help start any paper in a more thoughtful manner.

## 6   Freewriting to Find Ideas

Freewriting is writing quickly without worrying about rules. To freewrite, deliberately write as fast as possible and free-associate, allowing one word to trigger the next and one idea to lead to another. Ideas happen when you write intensely, nonstop, and without censoring, drawing thoughts from wherever in your mind they may reside. If you haven't freewritten before, the following suggestions will help.

- Write fast for a fixed period of time, say, ten minutes, on whatever problem needs solving or topic needs finding.

- Write the whole ten minutes without stopping to check spelling or word choice, stare at the ceiling, or think. So long as you continue writing, the words will generate the thoughts.

- Write to yourself. Don't worry about digressing or writing something silly. If you catch a new thought while writing even silly things, the freewriting has done its job.

To focus this technique, try a sequence of freewrites, each one starting with the most interesting sentence in the last freewrite, then looping back in on itself to push your idea ever deeper.

- Freewrite for ten minutes on a possible paper topic.

- Review your freewrite. Select one sentence, copy it to a fresh sheet of paper, and freewrite for another ten minutes.

- Repeat as often as necessary to locate your topic.

## 7   Journal Writing to Explore Ideas

Journals are personal notebooks that allow writers to explore their own thoughts and feelings about anything that matters. Instructors commonly ask you to keep a journal to help you focus on the subject matter of a single discipline but also to speculate broadly on the whole range of your academic experience. A journal differs from other academic assignments in that it is written primarily for yourself, not the professor. Like diaries, journals are written in the first person ("I") about ideas related to a college subject that are important to the writer. Here are some guidelines for writing a successful journal.

- Date each entry.
- Use your natural voice (as in freewriting).
- Write regularly (several times a week if not daily).

Above all, journals are discovery and practice books in which you are free to try out new ideas. A well-kept journal will be the best possible record of your educational experience. The following suggestions will make journal writing useful in any college class.

- Explore potential topics, try sample introductions, make possible arguments, record relevant research, assess progress, and make plans for what to do next.
- Ask questions as you write: What's my point? What's missing? How might my argument be made stronger?
- Use a loose-leaf notebook so you can share relevant entries with your instructor while continuing to write in it for yourself.
- Look for connections between academic and personal knowledge.
- Responding informally in your journal to assigned readings will help you remember them better. What was the author's point? What interested me most?

# 8    Clustering to See Ideas

Clustering is a method of listing ideas in a nonlinear way to reveal the relationships among them. Clustering is useful for both discovering and exploring a topic after you have done preliminary research. Like outlining, the act of clustering helps you invent and organize at the same time. To create a clustering diagram, follow this procedure:

■ Write a word or phrase that seems to focus on what you want to write about. For example, write "acid rain" in the middle of a page and circle it.

■ Connect supporting ideas to your circled phrase by drawing a line from the phrase to the related concepts. Circle and connect each aspect of acid rain back to the central idea.

■ To expand further, draw possible clusters from each of the subclusters, in this way finding ever more detailed ideas to work with.

## 9  Outlining to Organize Ideas

Outlines are organized lists. They are a powerful way to begin and advance a writing project—so long as you understand that you can modify the outline when new and better ideas emerge. To make an outline, start with an idea, and then see how many questions you can ask about it. If you start with "acid rain," ask, *What is it? What causes it? What are its effects? How can it be stopped?* Once you have such a list, arrange answers in a progression that makes sense, throwing out those that don't fit and adding others as they seem relevant.

Formal outlines follow a few guidelines to establish hierarchy (major versus minor ideas) and logic (which ideas depend on which). Use Roman numerals for major headings, Arabic *capital letters* for supporting ones, and Arabic *numbers* for still smaller ideas. Keep parallel ideas in parallel grammatical form (e.g., use all noun clusters or all complete sentences, but be consistent).

In the following example, the four main points are designated with Roman numerals; the supporting ideas, with Arabic capital letters; and the smaller details, with Arabic numbers.

I.   *Definition of acid rain*
II.  *Causes of acid rain*
   A.   *Coal-burning power plants*
      1.   *Power-generating stations*
      2.   *Steel mills*
      3.   *Factories*
   B.   *Automobile pollution*
III. *Effects of acid rain*
   A.   *Deforestation in New England*
   B.   *Dead lakes*
IV.  *Solutions to the acid rain problem*

The effort to make an outline not only helps organize the paper but also shows you what you don't know and where your supporting information is weak. Outlining at the beginning helps shape direction; outlining in the middle helps retain or reshape direction. Don't be afraid to modify or scrap initial outlines when your thoughts take you in new and better directions.

# 10 Asking Reporter's Questions to Test Ideas

Writers who train themselves to ask questions are also training themselves to find information. Reporters train themselves to ask six basic questions: Who? What? Where? When? Why? How? Using these questions will help you discover information. To generate topics about issues, events, or personal experience, ask yourself the reporter's questions:

- Who was involved?
- What happened?
- Where did this happen?
- When did it happen?
- Why did it happen?
- How did it happen?

Asking these questions about a first or second draft will tell you if you have included all the relevant information or left something out. In other words, it helps to ask reporter's questions both at the beginning and at the end of your writing.

# Writing College Papers

Academic papers are assigned for a variety of purposes that vary according to discipline, instructor, situation, and writer intention. Whether a paper presents information, explains ideas, supports a thesis, or explores ideas, the form, organization, style, and mechanics should be consistent with that purpose. The only guarantee of logical and formal consistency in academic papers is careful revision (see Chapters 14 and 15).

# 11 Finding Direction in Academic Papers

Purpose shapes a writer's questions, approach, research, organizing strategies, form, and voice. For the sake of brevity, we look at three common purposes behind college papers: *informing, persuading,* and *expressing.* But note that writing any paper often includes multiple purposes, all of which may not be discussed here. For example, while the larger intent of a paper may be persuasion, you may want to include expressive or informative passages to help accomplish that end.

## 11a. Writing to inform

Informative writing can be about any subject—literary, historical, and philosophical ideas; the results of laboratory and survey experiments; how-to demonstrations; and so on. The focus is on *information* rather than on *audience* or *writer;* consequently, the language in such reports is usually neutral, excluding personal opinion, bias, and first-person pronouns as much as possible. Standard strategies of presenting information include explaining, defining, describing, classifying and dividing, comparing and contrasting, and analyzing causes and effects. Common forms include laboratory and book reports as well as research papers.

- An informational report usually reveals its purpose in its title and in the introduction on the first page. If the report includes an informational thesis, that too is usually revealed on the first page. Such papers sometimes include an abstract after the title page, summarizing the paper's main points. This up-front focus on purpose helps readers home in on the information being presented.

## 11b. Writing to persuade

Persuasive writing attempts to convince readers that one idea, interpretation, product, or argument is better than another. An effective persuasive paper convinces the reader that the writer's claim is true. The information and personal beliefs expressed in it assure your reader that what you say has merit. Persuasive papers are among the most frequently assigned college papers; they ask you to argue, interpret, convince, defend, debate, or make a case for or against something. Forms include position papers, critical or interpretive essays, editorials, reviews, and any paper that requires taking a stand and backing it up.

■ Persuasion or argument papers commonly include a thesis that directly and succinctly states the author's main point. The thesis statement sometimes comes at the beginning (the rest of the paper supports it) or sometimes is delayed until the end (both sides have now been examined, and one is more persuasive than the other).

## 11c.  Writing to express

Expressive or personal writing reveals how the author thinks or feels about something and commonly raises more questions than it answers. Formally assigned papers that invite authors to express their personal ideas are often called *essays* (from the French verb *essayer,* "to attempt") that explore, speculate about, or reflect on a given question, issue, or text. Such expressive essays commonly focus as much on the quality of the *writer's* mind and voice as on the *subject* or *audience.* The meaning or point of such essays is as likely to be speculative or ambiguous as conclusive.

■ Expressive essays commonly examine, explore, or imply a thesis rather than state or support one in a definitive manner.

## 12  Making Claims in Academic Papers

The reason for writing academic papers is often to answer questions that are either stated or implied. Even a simple report explaining the principle of "lift" on airplane wings answers a question about how airplanes fly. An interpretive essay arguing in favor of cultural diversity answers a question about the value of cultural diversity. In many college papers, both in English and across the curriculum, the answer to such questions is called a *thesis*. If you are required to write a thesis-driven paper, make sure you know what a thesis is, where you want it to appear, and how to state it in a convincing manner.

## 12a. Thesis statements

Although the whole text of a sharply focused paper explains or argues its thesis, both informative and argument papers benefit from stating the paper's main point in a single sentence, called a **thesis statement.** Articulating your thesis on the first page makes clear to readers where the paper is going and what the rest of the paper will explain, argue, support, or defend. Articulating the thesis at the paper's end after exploring both sides of an issue leaves no doubt about where you stand.

When you begin to write, it helps to formulate a **working thesis** to focus your quest for an answer. As you research and write, both your question and your thesis may change—a good sign, because it means that you are learning something you didn't already know. For example, to begin writing a paper on cultural diversity, you might ask this question:

- **Question:** *How can Northfield College attract more minority students to increase cultural diversity on campus?*

To address this question—to which you do not know the answer—you make a good guess, which we'll call a *hypothesis* or *working thesis.* Your guess should (1) suggest a possible real answer and (2) be doable in the time and with the resources available. Make this tentative assertion as specific as your current knowledge allows.

- **Working thesis:** *To attract minority students, Northfield College needs to create a more culturally diverse campus environment.*

At this point in starting the paper, you have only a hunch about what the answer might be. Further research, however, convinces you that faculty diversity is the key to student diversity, so your paper's final thesis becomes the following:

■ **Thesis statement:** *Northfield College will attract minority students if it hires minority faculty to teach them.*

A good strategy for academic papers is to include the thesis statement on the first page, preferably at the end of a first paragraph that poses the problem the paper will address. In this way, your instructor knows right away the purpose of your paper and will read to see if that purpose is achieved. Here, for example, is the first paragraph for the Northfield College paper:

> Recent racial incidents among students in the dormitories at Northfield College have called attention to the homogeneous nature of the students, who, like the faculty, are largely white and of European ancestry. Current students, supported by the trustees and faculty, have called for increased efforts to recruit minority students in the belief that this would decrease racial tension. But how are minority students to be recruited to an all-white campus? This paper argues that Northfield College will attract more minority students if it hires minority faculty to teach them.

## 12b.  Claims and counterclaims

The main point made by academic papers is called a thesis (stated or implied), but it could also be called its major **claim.** Likewise, each point in support of that overall claim can be called a minor claim. Simply put, a claim is an assertion or statement that something is true or should be done. This chapter proposes a simple process for making and sequencing claims; the following section explains how to support them.

### Finding a topic

A common academic assignment requires you to write an argument or position paper about a controversial topic or issue. Start this paper by selecting an issue that interests you and that also meets the following criteria:

■ It is controversial.

■ It has two distinct, arguable, and realistic positions.

■ Resources are available to support both sides.

Consider the difference between national versus local topics: National topics, such as homeland security or universal health care, are widely reported in the major news media and well documented in the university library and on the Internet. Local topics, such as mountain biking in Riverside Park or cultural diversity at Northfield College, will provide places to visit and experts to interview. Our sample topic is both national (mountain biking in wilderness areas) and local (a proposal to ban mountain biking in Riverside Park)—a guarantee of rich and varied research sources:

- Should mountain biking be allowed in Riverside Park?

## Making claims

Once you've selected an issue and chosen which side to support, use research and careful reasoning to make a list of all the claims that support your side of the argument—you're not writing the paper yet, just preparing the outline. Here, for example, are the claims to support mountain biking in Riverside Park:

- All people should have the right to use the park so long as they do not damage it.
- A Sierra Club study found that mountain bike tires are less harmful to forest trails than lug-soled hiking boots.
- Most mountain bike riders are respectful of the environment and courteous to other trail users.

## Making counterclaims

Statements that present the other side of an issue are called **counterclaims.** Once the claims are listed, list the counterclaims that challenge your position:

- Mountain bike riders ride fast and are sometimes reckless.
- Mountain bike tires damage trails and cause erosion.

After listing the counterclaims, you can conclude your paper by refuting them or arguing that your claims are more valid.

## Writing the paper

Before you finish writing this position paper, you have one more strategic decision to make: Do you want to lead with your thesis so that readers know where you stand from the start, or do you want to delay stating your thesis and keep the readers in suspense?

There are three advantages to leading with a thesis: (1) The audience always knows where you stand. (2) The thesis occupies both emphatic positions in a paper, first and last. (3) Thesis-first is the expected form of academic argument in many disciplines.

There are also three advantages to a delayed-thesis argument: (1) You show your audience both sides of the issue. (2) Being kept in suspense increases reader interest in finishing the paper. (3) The audience understands your difficulty in making a decision.

## 13    Using Evidence in Academic Writing

When you write papers that make claims about what is true, the following sources can be counted on to provide believable evidence: *facts, examples, inferences, expert opinion,* and *personal experience.*

**Facts** are verifiable and agreed on by everyone, regardless of personal beliefs or values. It is a fact that water boils at 212 degrees Fahrenheit. It is a fact that Northfield College employed three black faculty members in 2004. It is a fact that Riverside Park is adjacent to the western boundary of the college campus. Facts are often numerical or statistical and are recorded where readers can look them up in a dictionary, almanac, public report, college catalog, or atlas.

"Near facts" may be another category that most reasonable people would subscribe to, although means of proof are more questionable: Mount Hood is a tall mountain, Milwaukee is a large city, French is a romantic language.

**Examples** illustrate a claim or clarify an issue. To explain that many wilderness trails remain closed to mountain biking, report those so listed by the National Park Service.

**Inferences** are generalizations based on the accumulation of a certain number of facts and examples. For instance, if you check three city parks and find that they are all open to mountain biking, you might infer a city policy supporting that sport in city parks. But such an inference is not a fact because you have not checked all the city parks or checked with the department that sets park policies.

**Expert opinion** makes powerful evidence. When a forest ranger testifies about trail damage caused by mountain bikes or lug-soled hiking boots, his training and experience make him an expert. A casual hiker making the same observation is less believable.

**Personal experience** is testimony based on firsthand knowledge. If you have ridden mountain bikes in Riverside Park for two years, your knowledge cannot easily be discounted.

# 14 Guidelines for Revision

Learning to write is learning to rewrite, which happens in two distinct stages: (1) **revising,** the primary way of developing a paper's ideas and direction, and (2) **editing,** the primary way of polishing and refining its sentences (the final stage of editing, **proofreading,** detects errors in spelling, typing, grammar, and punctuation).

Revising means seeing the topic, thesis, claims, evidence, organization, or conclusion through new eyes and making changes to modify the paper's content, direction, and meaning. There is no single way to revise, but the following strategies may help.

- Compose all drafts on a computer so that you can add, delete, and move blocks of text easily before you are done.

- Create self-imposed due dates earlier than the instructor's due date to guarantee you'll have time to revise and edit.

- Let a first draft sit overnight; the next day, you'll see more clearly what works well, what doesn't, and where to make changes.

- If you make a change in one place, it may have repercussions elsewhere in the paper. Review everything.

- Ask readers you trust about the strength of your thesis, the credibility of your evidence, and the clarity of your point.

- Read your paper out loud. Does it sound like you—your commitments and voice? If not, revise until it does.

- Sticking with tedious topics, false directions, or old language hinders creative and critical thinking. Be willing to scrap and start fresh.

## 15 Experiments with Revision

You can bring new life to a paper by challenging yourself to see it in new ways. Consider these possibilities for re-focusing your work: (1) *Limit* focus or scope, (2) *add* new material, (3) *switch* perspective, and (4) *transform* the genre. These experiments work equally well with informative, persuasive, and expressive papers.

### Limit

Early drafts often cover too much ground in too few pages so that depth, detail, and development are lost.

- Limit your second draft to one idea in a single paragraph of your first draft.

- Limit your second draft to "real time" so that the action in your paper happens in the time it takes to read it.

- Limit your second draft to a single setting in which meaningful dialogue or action occurs.

### Add

Drafts get stale when writers keep rehashing the same ideas. Make a resolution to add new information with each revision.

- Add local people. Find a local expert to interview and quote in your paper.

- Add re-created dialogue by visualizing an experience and employing language that approximates the occasion.

■ Add library and Internet sources to teach readers more than you knew when you started writing.

## Switch

Revitalize drafts by switching your point of view. You don't need to stay "switched" for more than a draft, but this experiment lets you witness the story afresh.

■ Switch point of view (first versus third person), verb tense (past versus present), style, or voice (formal versus colloquial) to present your ideas from a different perspective.

■ Switch audience by writing a draft to a distant friend to see how changing audience changes your language.

■ Switch from exposition to narrative or vice versa. Narrate the story of your search instead of simply reporting its results.

## Transform

Experiment with a new form or genre. You will not know the full effect of a new form until you actually create it; it might be a pleasant surprise.

■ Transform within nonfiction genres: Rewrite a personal essay as a journal, diary, or letter exchange. Recast a research paper as a feature article or as talk-show dialogue.

■ Transform to creative genres: Instead of prose, write verse; instead of narrative, write drama.

■ Transform to a form that complements and enhances the content of the paper.

When you try any of these experiments, treat the content of the paper just as seriously as if you wrote in a more conventional mode. To be safe, check with your instructor before turning in a creative final draft.

# Editing for Clarity

Careful editing answers the following questions:

- Does my introduction catch the reader's attention? (Chapter 17)
- Is my main point (or thesis) clearly stated? (Chapter 12)
- Does my conclusion produce the right effect? (Chapter 18)
- Does one paragraph lead logically to the next? (Chapter 16)
- Are my sentences interesting and varied? (Chapter 19)
- Are my sentences clear, direct, and economical? (Chapters 19–21)
- Is my language matched to my audience? (Chapters 22–24)

# 16   Effective Paragraphs

Good paragraphing helps readers follow an author's ideas throughout a piece of writing by grouping related ideas in logical ways. When a new paragraph begins, readers expect a new idea or direction. They expect that within a paragraph, each sentence will help develop or advance a main idea—that the paragraph will be *unified*. Readers also expect that each paragraph will present its ideas in an order that makes sense—that it will be *organized*. And they expect that each sentence within a paragraph will relate clearly to the sentences around it—that it will be *coherent*.

When drafting, writers often break into new paragraphs intuitively at places where they leave one thought and begin another or where a break seems needed. So even though there are no hard and fast rules to cover every reason to paragraph, it is a good idea to review your intuitive paragraphing to see that it helps rather than confuses readers.

## 16a.   Unity

To edit for paragraph unity, first determine the paragraph's main idea or topic; keep words and sentences that support or clarify that main idea, and delete or move those that do not. In practice, how you determine the unifying principle for any given paragraph depends on the amount of information, your larger organizing principle, and the point you want to make. Keep things together that you think your audience needs to see together.

Writing a **topic sentence** at the beginning or end of a paragraph can state the unifying principle clearly and can help readers find information or follow an argument. In writing based on experience or reflection, however, paragraph topics may be implied rather than stated.

## 16b.   Order

Ideas presented in no apparent order confuse readers. To organize information within paragraphs, a topic sentence helps, but so do predictable patterns. Which one you choose depends on what you are trying to do. The following patterns are so well known that readers will follow them easily, but other organizing ideas work as well.

**General to specific.** Begin with a general statement and then move to examples that support, explain, and expand it: *Start with an idea about kitchens and then move to what's in them—stoves, refrigerators, microwave ovens, and so on.*

**Specific to general.** Start with a series of details and culminate in a general statement: *Start with stoves, microwave ovens, and refrigerators; conclude with the kitchen.* Placing your general statement at the end emphasizes the larger category.

**Chronological.** Present events in the order in which they happened: *First talk about the fog, then the rain, and finally the sun.* The topic sentence can appear at the beginning or at the end of the paragraph.

**Reverse chronological.** Move backward from the most recent events to the most distant: *today, last week, a year ago.* This is an effective way to reflect on the past or to trace the causes of events.

**Climactic order.** Use suspense to build toward a conclusion: *Begin with a goal, follow with difficulties, and conclude with victory.*

**Spatial.** Lead the viewer's imagination from one concrete object to another: *First focus on the door, then the window, then the chair, and finally the note on the table.* Build toward a complete picture or an event.

To test which pattern is best, let your word processor help: (1) Insert returns so that each sentence begins on a new line; rearrange sentences until you find the best organization. (2) Use the copy function to make several copies of the same paragraph; organize the paragraph in several different ways; then compare and choose the best one for your situation.

## 16c.   Coherence

A paragraph coheres—"sticks together"—when each sentence in it relates appropriately to the surrounding sentences. Use *transitional expressions (however, furthermore, at the same time, meanwhile)* to connect or contrast ideas, show relationships in time and space, or suggest cause and effect.

**Break long paragraphs.** Long paragraphs, no matter how coherent, strain readers' attention. Look for places to break long paragraphs into shorter paragraphs, but find a way to connect the related material.

**Combine short paragraphs.** A string of very short paragraphs can make ideas seem disconnected. Look for places where like material in separate paragraphs can be combined into more substantial paragraphs, or flesh out the short paragraphs with more information.

**Repeat key words.** Strategically repeating key words emphasizes a main idea and makes it easier for readers to follow your thoughts.

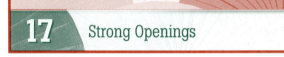

## 17    Strong Openings

The first words of your paper must engage your readers, introduce your topic and your main idea, and point toward what you intend to say. In a two- or three-page essay, one paragraph may suffice to open; in longer papers, you may have a page or two to play with. The following techniques make openings more engaging.

**Open with a thesis statement.** Many opening paragraphs in college papers start with a broad general statement, narrow the focus, and end by stating the thesis.

> Women's basketball is the television sport of the future.

**Open with a striking assertion.** Make a statement so bold that the reader will demand to see proof.

> Inch for inch, women are better basketball players than men.

**Open with an anecdote.** Use a brief story to introduce the topic and illustrate the thesis.

> When Jenny Wilkins was ten years old, she was five feet tall and could vertically jump four feet.

**Open with an interesting detail, statistic, or quotation.** Plunge readers into an unfamiliar situation to pique their curiosity.

> Within ten years, personal flying machines will be found in many suburban backyards.

**Open with a provocative question.** Introduce your thesis as a question. After a few sentences of background information, state your thesis as an answer to that question.

> What would the world be like without any insects?

**Avoid broad, worn-out generalizations.** Readers find them boring rather than enticing.

> Modern society is a rat race.

## 18     Thoughtful Closings

An effective concluding paragraph leaves readers satisfied with the discussion and gives them something to think about or act on. It also reminds readers of your main idea or thesis. You can develop a statement or restatement of the main idea in one of several ways.

**Carry your thesis one step further.** Perhaps your argument is so strong that your conclusion can go beyond your initial thesis.

> Despite the military's objections, soldiers will continue to take on peacekeeping work. In fact, experience has shown that peacekeeping and nation-building will play a vital role in foreign policy for years to come.

**Close with a rhetorical question.** Such a question is not to be answered but to persuade the reader to agree with you.

> How can concerned citizens stand by and do nothing?

**Close with a genuine question.** State honestly that you don't have all the answers.

What will happen to the American economy when all the oil reserves are gone?

**Close with a concise summary.** Repeat the important points in the paper.

Northfield College needs to recruit minority faculty actively and at the same time educate the student body about multicultural issues.

**Close with a call to action.** Use your powers of persuasion to mobilize readers to action.

It's time for all of us to eat more carefully, walk more deliberately, and slow down.

**Close with speculation.** Imagine the future if the action you propose is—or is not—taken.

If we don't ban the use of cell phones in rush hour traffic, even more accidents will happen.

## 19  Sentence Variety

Reading a paper in which all the sentences have the same structure and length can be tedious. Early drafts sometimes come out this way. However, if you understand how sentences are constructed, it's easy to edit them into engaging patterns. Use *coordination, subordination,* and *parallelism* to restructure your sentences to create more lively reading. First, let's review sentence types.

A **simple sentence** has a single independent clause—at least a subject and a verb or, more commonly, a subject, verb, and object.

$$\overset{S}{\text{John}} \overset{V}{\text{ran.}}$$

$$\overset{S}{\text{Pollution is}} \overset{V}{\text{a growing}} \overset{O}{\text{problem.}}$$

A **compound sentence** has two or more independent clauses joined either by a comma and a coordinating conjunction or by a semicolon.

Pollution is a problem, and it won't go away soon.

Recycling will help; it saves on landfill space.

A **complex sentence** has one independent clause and one or more dependent clauses.

Because the problem continues to grow, our legislature must act before it is too late.

A **compound-complex sentence** has at least two independent clauses and one or more dependent clauses.

Pollution can be prevented, and we must take action to stop it because there is no other way to survive on this planet.

## 19a.  Coordinate structures

To specify a relationship, connect two independent clauses with one of the seven coordinating conjunctions, *for, and, nor, but, or, yet, so* (to help you remember these seven words, note that their first letters, in this order, spell "*fanboys*").

We had eggs for breakfast, and then we went for a walk.

Avoid using coordination where the meaning of the two sentences is not related closely enough to warrant joining them.

I made eggs for breakfast, and I missed the bus.

## 19b.  Subordinate structures

To emphasize one idea and deemphasize another, place one in a subordinate (less important) relationship to the other. In the following simple sentences, two ideas are presented as roughly equal.

John Playford collected seventeenth-century music. He was an English musician.

To emphasize Playford's activity (first sentence), subordinate his identification (second sentence) in a phrase set off by commas.

John Playford, an English musician, collected seventeenth-century music.

To emphasize Playford's identity, subordinate his activity.

John Playford, who collected seventeenth-century music, was an English musician.

The place of greatest emphasis in a sentence is usually the end.

# 19c. Parallel structures

Parallelism means repeating the same structure to highlight a comparison or to emphasize a point. In the following examples, notice how parallelism creates a pleasing rhythm.

### PARALLEL WORDS

Few devices impart greater *power, gravity,* and *impact* than a well-constructed parallel.

### PARALLEL PHRASES

Ours is a government of the people, by the people, and for the people.

### PARALLEL CLAUSES

The question is not whether the town will plan to have no growth but whether it will face growth with no plan.

Parallel constructions are powerful because they are rhythmic and memorable. The secret to parallelism's power lies in pairing identical grammatical structures.

Instead of settling for "*Laura likes painting and writing and likes to read,*" make the constructions match: "*Laura likes painting, writing, and reading.*"

Instead of "*Wind energy is not only difficult to capture but also costs a lot to store,*" make the second phrase match the first: "*Wind energy is not only difficult to capture but also expensive to store.*"

# 20    Concise Wording

Academic, business, and technical writing should convey information clearly and efficiently. Edit to express ideas with no wasted words. Write concisely, and you'll avoid being vague, wordy, obscure, or confusing.

## 20a.  Vague generalities

Generalizations are broad statements without specific detail that express large concepts and abstractions—components especially necessary to academic writing. Sometimes, however, writers make too many general unsupported statements that have been repeated so often they pack no power: *It is our duty today to take responsibility for our actions.* (How many times have you been told that?)

Other times the generality is so widely accepted that stating it seems silly: *Shakespeare is a great writer.* (Yes?)

Some generalities indulge in circular reasoning: *During the harsh winters of the 1870s, the weather was very cold.* (*Harsh* implies that.)

Others announce that a point is going to be made but don't make it: *Many factors played a part in the President's victory.* (What factors?)

Although generalities can occur anywhere, look carefully at your openings and conclusions, where you may be trying hard to impress. Look for the obvious and edit it out:

> Fetal alcohol syndrome affects one of every 750 newborn babies. ~~It is clearly not good for them~~, causing coordination problems, malformed organs, small brains, short attention spans, and behavioral problems.

## 20b.  Idle words

People use many unnecessary words when they talk. Writers of first drafts also digress and ramble as they explore what they really want to say. Careful editing helps them convey their thoughts more precisely.

> To edit ~~very~~ wordy drafts, test each ~~and every~~ word to see if eliminating it ~~tightens the expression and makes it more concise or~~ changes the meaning. If the meaning is ~~ultimately~~ unchanged, ~~consider~~ drop~~ping~~ the word.

## 20c.  Automatic phrases

Phrases like *in my opinion, it has come to my attention that,* and *due to the fact that* contribute nothing to a discussion. They are a writer's "throat clearing." Such automatic phrases often appear at the beginnings of sentences, but look for them anywhere. When you find an automatic phrase, remove it and reread the passage. If no meaning is lost, leave it out. If some meaning seems to be missing, try condensing the phrase.

> ~~In this day and age~~, children ~~in many instances~~
> know more about black holes than they do about
> Black Beauty.

*(Today)* *(often)*

## 20d.  Wordy phrases

Vague, abstract nouns—*area, aspect, factor, kind, manner, nature, tendency, thing,* and *type*—may signal that wordiness is afoot. Often you can delete imprecise phrases, condense them, or find more concrete substitutes. If you ever write a sentence such as "*One of the factors that caused problems in the lab was the tendency toward contamination,*" change it to something more direct: "*Contamination was a problem in the lab*" or "*The lab was contaminated.*"

## 20e.  Useless modifiers

Writers often use modifiers such as *clearly, obviously, interestingly, undoubtedly, absolutely, fortunately, hopefully, really, totally,* and *very* to make a sentence sound forceful or authoritative. In truth, a sentence usually sounds stronger if these adverbs are taken out and the verb stands by itself.

> These intensifiers ~~clearly~~ add ~~very~~ little, and they
> can ~~hopefully~~ be deleted.

## 20f.  Redundancy

Public speakers are often advised, "Tell them what you're going to say, say it, and then tell them what you said." In speaking, repetition helps listeners understand. In writing, however, where readers are able to slow down, reread, and pause as they please, repetition is redundant unless it serves other purposes—to create emphasis and rhythm, for instance. As you edit, evaluate each instance of repetition. Ask whether the repetition links ideas, sustains an established rhythm, or prevents confusion. If not, cut it.

> The ~~general~~ consensus ~~of opinion~~ among students
> was that the chancellor had exceeded her authority.

*About ninety percent*
~~A very high percentage~~ of the prison's inmates take advantage of the special education program~~, about ninety percent~~.

# 20g.  Elliptical constructions

By omitting words that readers can be expected to supply for themselves, an elliptical construction helps avoid unneeded repetition. Such constructions are usually used in the second part of a parallel construction, where the first verb is implied for the second as well.

> Her words suggested one thing, ~~while~~ her actions ~~suggested~~ another.

# 20h.  Pretentious language

It is tempting, when you want to sound authoritative, to use technical, obscure, or ornate language. When such language is needlessly complicated or overinflated, it is called pretentious. Pretentious language uses two or three words where one would do and sometimes relies on the third-person point of view and the passive voice. Edit such constructions to find concrete subjects for your verbs and to address your readers more directly; rewriting is usually in order because crossing out existing language is seldom enough.

**ORIGINAL**

The range of audiovisual services provided includes examinations to determine optical or auditory impairment.

**EDITED**

We offer eye and ear examinations.

# 20i.  Euphemisms

A *euphemism* is an inoffensive word or phrase deliberately substituted for one considered harsh or indelicate. Our conversations are full of euphemisms, especially those that deal with money, death, sex, and body functions. Workers are fired in massive layoffs, but the company calls it *downsizing*. A person whose grandmother has died says, "*I lost my grandmother.*"

In academic writing, you strive to inform, not to obscure, but you must balance directness with your audience's comfort. If in doubt, ask a peer or an instructor to check your choices.

| **21** | Strong Verbs |

Verbs make things happen. They make the subjects (nouns) of sentences *race, run, erupt, scoot, shoot, dive, fly, climb, sprawl, meander, wonder,* and *ponder* and make your writing come alive.

## 21a. Replace static verbs with action verbs

Verbs drive sentences the way an engine powers a car. Action verbs—verbs that denote specific actions—add horsepower. Static verbs that show no action—*be, appear, become, seem, exist*—can leave your sentences underpowered. Replace static verbs with action verbs when you can.

> This problem will soon ~~become evident~~ *erupt*.

A form of *be* preceding a phrase or a clause often signals a stronger verb coming up. Make this verb the main verb of the sentence.

> The most effective writers ~~are those who~~ write as though they were simply talking.

Stronger verbs are often hidden in parts of sentences beginning with constructions such as *there are, there is,* and *it is.* In these cases, turn the verb of the clause into the main verb of the sentence.

> ~~There are m~~*M*any people ~~who~~ believe that Elvis Presley is still alive, even though ~~it is~~ only the tabloids ~~that~~ take such so-called news seriously.

## 21b. Avoid weak action verbs

Not all verbs that describe action spark clear images. Overuse has exhausted the image-making power of verbs such as *do, get, go, have, make,* and *think.* As you edit, watch for weak action verbs and substitute stronger verbs where possible.

He ~~makes~~ *bakes* good sourdough bread.

Often a verb that relies on other words for its descriptive power can be replaced with a more effective one.

He ~~walked quickly~~ *scurried* from the room.

## 21c.   Change nouns back to verbs

Many English verbs have been changed into useful nouns with the help of a suffix—*announce/announcement* or *tempt/temptation,* for example. Nouns made from verbs (called *nominalizations*) often bury the real action of a sentence. To make matters worse, these nouns usually require a static verb—*have, do, make,* or *be.* As you edit, dig up the buried verbs to resurrect your point.

Few biographies of FDR ~~have given a explanation of~~ *clearly explain* the disastrous Yalta conference.

To enliven your writing, replace these common expressions with the action verbs buried within them.

| NOMINAL EXPRESSION | BURIED VERB |
|---|---|
| put forth a proposal | propose |
| hold a discussion | discuss |
| formulate a plan | plan |
| reach a decision | decide |
| arrive at a conclusion | conclude |
| hold a meeting | meet |
| make a choice | choose |

## 21d.   Change passive voice to active

When a verb is in the active voice, the person or thing performing the action is the subject, which is the most natural, economical, and direct form of English expression.

| actor | active-voice verb | direct object (recipient of action) |
|---|---|---|
| Juana | collects | the tickets. |

When a verb is in the passive voice, the recipient of the action becomes the subject, and there is no object.

Passive-voice sentences are less economical and more in-direct and can take longer for readers to unravel.

| subject of action | passive-voice verb | agent of action |
|:---|:---|:---|
| The tickets | are collected | by Juana. |

## Favor the active voice

By focusing on the actor, the active voice helps readers visualize what happens and who does it. Active-voice sentences usually use fewer words and have a more di-rect effect than passive-voice sentences. (The sentences in this paragraph and the majority throughout this book are in the active voice.)

Use the active voice in most situations. Ideally, the subject of a sentence—what it's about—should be the gram-matical subject, and the action of the sentence should be expressed by the main verb.

> **PASSIVE**
> The candidate was surrounded by a throng of admirers who demanded a chance to talk with her.

> **ACTIVE**
> A throng of admirers surrounded the candidate, demanding a chance to talk with her.

## When to use the passive voice

The passive voice deemphasizes the actor and highlights the recipient of the verb's action—an effect you may choose for selected occasions such as the following.

> **TO STRESS RESULTS**
> A $500 million reduction in the national debt was approved by Congress.

> **TO LEAVE THE AGENT UNSTATED**
> A new homeless shelter was established in a vacant warehouse.

> **TO SUGGEST OBJECTIVITY**
> The samples were tested for bacteria.

# 22 Specific Nouns and Modifiers

Compare the mental picture you get from the phrase *an old car* versus the phrase *a rusted baby-blue 1959 Buick*. The first phrase evokes no specific image; the second phrase calls up a specific car for readers to visualize. When sentences contain specific, identifiable "characters" such as the blue Buick, they tell small stories that readers recognize and enter into.

**Abstract words** refer to ideas and concepts that cannot be perceived by the senses: *transportation, wealth, childhood, nutrition*. **Concrete words** name things that can be seen, felt, heard, tasted, or smelled: *a dime, Robert, broccoli, mahogany*.

**General words** refer to categories and groups: *pets, stores, teachers, cars*. **Specific words** identify objects or people: *Rover, Murphy's Drugs, Pauline Clay, the 1959 Buick*.

## 22a.  Concrete, specific nouns

We would be unable to think, speak, or write about literature, constitutionality, or music without terms to name these abstract ideas. However, writing that relies exclusively on abstractions seems like nothing but hot air. To give form, shape, and life to the abstract and general, look for specific details and examples.

Campus radicalism increased in the 1960s and 1970s.
*like the one at Kent State University in Ohio*
Protests and antiwar demonstrations were common.
                                                ^

## 22b.  Specific modifiers

Choose modifiers (words and phrases that describe nouns and verbs) that are specific and concrete. Look for modifiers that appeal to any of the reader's five senses: *red* peppers, *whispered* words, *hot* stove, *juicy* peaches, *oily* skin.

Some descriptive modifiers have become empty and meaningless through overuse; be wary of writing any of these too often: *pretty, dull, dumb, nice, beautiful, good, bad, young, old, great, fantastic, terrible, awesome, awful.* The intensifier *very* can be one of the worst offenders.

Madeline was a ~~very pretty~~ girl with ~~nice~~ brown eyes.

## 23 | The Right Word

The English language has a particularly rich vocabulary. The place you live, for instance, might be your *house, home, residence, abode, dwelling, domicile, habitation, quarters, lodging, apartment, pad, place, shack, spot,* or *digs.* It's your job as a writer to find the right word to convey your meaning.

Many writers rely on dictionaries and thesauruses to guide them in the use of language. These resources can sharpen your word skills and improve your writing.

### 23a. Roots, prefixes, and suffixes

Roots, prefixes, and suffixes provide clues to a word's meaning. A **root** is a base word, or part of a word, from which other words are formed: *mile* in the word *mileage,* for example.

A **prefix** is a group of letters attached before a root that changes its meaning: *un-* in *unfinished.* The word *prefix* itself consists of a root, *fix,* which means "attach," and a prefix, *pre-,* meaning "before." A **suffix** is a group of letters attached to the end of a root: *-age* in *mileage.*

Both prefixes and suffixes change the meaning of the root to which they are attached. For example, the words *antebellum, bellicose,* and *belligerent* share the root *bellum,* Latin for "war." If you already know that *belligerent* means "warlike or at war," you might guess that *antebellum* means "before [a particular] war."

### 23b. Denotations and connotations

The **denotation** of a word is its direct, literal meaning. *Fragrance, odor,* and *smell* denote the same thing: a perception detected by your olfactory sense. But the associations, or *connotations,* of the words differ. "*You have a distinct fragrance*" suggests a pleasant smell, whereas "*You have a distinct odor*" suggests an unpleasant one. The associated or indirect meaning of a word is its **connotation.** Edit carefully to eliminate unintended connotations.

## 23c.  Idiomatic expressions

Why do we ride *in* a car but *on* a train? Why do we *take* a picture but *make* a recording? Such conventional—that is, widely accepted—speech patterns are called **idioms,** patterns that may not follow rules of logic or grammar.

## 23d.  Slang, regionalisms, and colloquialism

Everyone uses **slang,** informal language that originates in and is unique to small groups such as students, musicians, athletes, or politicians. Some slang words eventually enter the mainstream and become part of standard English. A *jeep* was originally slang for a general-purpose (*g.p.*) military vehicle used in World War II. Now it is the brand name of a vehicle driven by many Americans.

**Regionalisms** are expressions used in one part of the country but not elsewhere. The name for a carbonated beverage, for example, varies by region from *pop* to *soda* to *soft drink* to *seltzer* to *phosphate*. Some bits of regional dialect are regarded as nonstandard, that is, not acceptable in academic writing.

A **colloquialism** is an expression common to spoken language but seldom used in formal writing. For example, nearly all speakers of American English would understand you if you said someone "*up and left the room,*" but you would be careful to write that the person "*got up and left*" or "*left suddenly.*"

Use slang words, regionalisms, and colloquialisms sparingly, if at all, in academic writing. They may not be understood, and their informality may imply a lack of rigor, discrimination, or care on your part. They can, however, convey immediacy and authenticity in descriptions and dialogue.

## 23e.  Jargon

Every profession or field develops terms to express its special ideas. Such specialized or technical language is called **jargon.**

As you edit, decide whether your audience will understand your terms. Using fewer technical terms helps you communicate better with a general audience, but a specialized audience expects you to use technical language appropriately. For example, for what kind of audience would you substitute *femur* for *thigh bone* or vice versa? Avoid jargon added merely to make your writing sound important.

## 23f.　Figurative language

**Figurative language,** which likens one thing to another in imaginative ways, brings freshness and resonance to writing. Well-crafted figurative language, often in the form of comparisons and analogies, can help readers gain insight.

One of the most common problems writers have is inadvertently juxtaposing incongruous images. A **mixed metaphor** combines two or more unrelated images, often with unintended effects. When you find a mixed metaphor in your writing, eliminate the weaker one and extend the more appropriate one.

> We must ~~fight~~ ^swim^ against the tide of cynicism that threatens to ~~cloud our vision~~ ^drown our hope^ of a world without hunger.

*Swim/tide/drown/hope* call up a more consistent and therefore clearer image than *fight/tide/cloud/vision.*

## 23g.　Clichés

Our language is full of overused, worn-out expressions called **clichés.** Although clichés convey images (which sounds like a good idea), the same image has been used so much that seeing or hearing it no longer conjures up an image in the reader's mind the way fresh images do. The following images have now become clichés—how many more can you think of?

| | |
|---|---|
| the last straw | needle in a haystack |
| sharp as a tack | handwriting on the wall |
| lay your cards on the table | toe the line |
| a drop in the bucket | hit the nail on the head |
| best thing since sliced bread | jump-start the economy |

When you notice you've used a cliché, replace it with a direct statement.

## 24   Unbiased Language

Academic discourse prizes open-mindedness and tolerance as basic requirements of inquiry and discovery. Careless word choice can make you sound ignorant or prejudiced.

Using a generalization about a group of people to predict, describe, or interpret the behavior or characteristics of an individual in that group is both illogical and insensitive. Careless generalizations based on race, ethnicity, gender, cultural background, age, physical characteristics, or lifestyles are called **stereotypes.** Whether they refer to gender, race, ethnicity, or sexual preference, stereotypes substitute a simplistic formula for an appreciation of individual differences and the richness of human variation.

## 24a.  Recognizing stereotypes

Many stereotypes stem from ignorance and from fear of people who are perceived as different. These stereotypes often penetrate our language both in descriptions of people—*liberal politician*—and in descriptive images—*sleepy Southern town.* Calling a doctor or a lawyer *he* without reference to a specific person reinforces the stereotype that all doctors or lawyers are men.

Edit your writing to eliminate stereotypes. Qualify broad generalizations, and support or replace sweeping statements with specific factual evidence. In some cases, drop the stereotypical observation altogether.

> Like most ~~teenage~~ ^*inexperienced*^ drivers, he was reckless.

> ~~Like so many of his race,~~ Shaquille O'Neal
>
> is a gifted athlete.

## 24b.  Choosing group labels

People often label themselves in terms of the groups to which they belong. However, labels inevitably emphasize a single feature of a person's identity, ignoring other characteristics. They also may offend people who do not want to be so characterized. Furthermore, many labels go beyond simple identification and become explicitly or implicitly derogatory. As you edit, examine any labels you have used; try to use only those acceptable to the members of the group themselves, and avoid labels with negative connotations.

## Designations of race, ethnicity, and nationality

The terms *black, African American,* and *people of color* are widely used. The term *African American* is both an adjective and a noun.

Many people of Asian ancestry prefer the term *Asian* or *Asian American* to the term *Oriental.* It is always correct to refer to an individual's or group's national origin: Japanese, Korean, Malaysian, Chinese, and so on.

Today, some Americans of Spanish-speaking heritage refer to themselves as *Hispanics;* others prefer *Latino* and *Latina,* and some Mexican Americans use *Chicano* and *Chicana.* Many *Native Americans* prefer that term to *Indian,* but using the name of the tribe or nation is often a better choice: Navajo, Lakota Sioux, Seneca. Some *Inuit* prefer that term to *Eskimo.*

## Designations of gender and sexual orientation

Most adult women prefer to be called *women* rather than *girls* or *ladies. Girl* is particularly inappropriate in reference to salespeople, administrative staff, or those in service jobs.

When writing about sexual orientation is appropriate to your purpose, keep in mind that people have widely different views about the role of sexuality in our personal and public lives. Be aware that not everyone may share your perspective, and consider using a group's or a person's own chosen term.

## Designations of ability

People with physical limitations often prefer *disabled* to *handicapped.* Some writers use *differently abled.*

## Designations of age

Use *elderly* or *aged* only in a general sense: *the elderly population.* If an individual's age is critical to what you want to say, cite the person's actual age: 68-year-old.

## Checking labels for negative connotations

Some labels that seem neutral may hide negative connotations. For example, the term *AIDS victims* implies that such people are blameless, which you may intend, but also that they are helpless, which you may not. *People with AIDS* is a more neutral choice.

# 24c.  Using nonsexist language

When you use words that embody gender stereotypes, you risk alienating large portions of your potential audience. Gender bias can arise from unexamined habits of thought and language.

## Pronoun choice

Until recently, *he, him,* and *his* were used generically to refer to singular nouns or pronouns whose gender was unknown, unstated, or irrelevant: *Anyone who believes those promises should have <u>his</u> head examined.* Such usage is disappearing because many people believe that the generic *he* excludes women.

However, English has no singular personal pronoun of indefinite gender to match the gender-neutral plural pronoun *they.* In speaking, people often use plural pronouns to avoid the masculine forms: *Everybody had fun on their vacations.* But in a sentence with a singular subject (*everybody*), any pronoun that refers to it should be singular, so you have to choose between <u>his</u> and <u>her.</u>

If you know the gender of the first reference, match it with the pronoun of the same gender: *Each nun makes <u>her</u> own bed.*

If you don't know the gender, choose one of these strategies:

1. Make the antecedent plural and adjust other agreement problems:

   All the <u>residents</u> make <u>their</u> own beds.

2. Use *his or her:*

   Each resident makes <u>his or her</u> own bed.

3. Eliminate the pronoun by restructuring the surrounding sentence or sentences: instead of

   Everyone has done <u>his</u> part,

   write

   Everyone has <u>helped.</u>

## Universal terms

The use of *man* and *mankind* to refer to the whole of humanity seems to ignore the female half of the species. As you edit, substitute more inclusive terms such as *humanity, the human race, humankind,* or *people.*

## Occupational terms

In choosing terms for an occupation, focus on the occupation, not the gender of the person who holds it. Few jobs are "naturally" held by either men or women. Avoid language that implicitly identifies an occupation with gender—that assumes that all flight attendants, nurses, secretaries, or teachers are female or all airline pilots, business executives, streetcar conductors, or bronco busters are male.

Avoid using occupational terms with feminine suffixes: *actress, authoress, poetess, executrix.* Such feminine forms have become obsolete, and the formerly male form has become neutral: *author, poet, actor, executor.* Others, such as *waitress,* are changing to more inclusive terms: *server* or *waitperson,* for example.

Occupational terms that end in *–man* imply that everyone who does that job is male. Gender-neutral substitutes for many occupations are available:

**CHECKLIST OF NEUTRAL OCCUPATIONAL LABELS**

| SEXIST | NEUTRAL |
| --- | --- |
| statesman | diplomat |
| mailman | letter carrier, mail carrier |
| policeman | police officer |
| fireman | firefighter |
| businessman | executive, businessperson |
| salesman | sales representative |
| councilman | council member |

## 24d.  Eliminating stereotypes

As you edit, ask these four questions:

1. Have I relied more on stereotypes than on evidence to make my point? Is the statement that "*African Americans are good dancers*" really true?

2. Do my generalizations follow logically from factual evidence? Or am I appealing to prejudice by suggesting that "*all _____ are like that*"?

**3.** Do my generalizations about a group improperly label individuals: Is it true that "*students these days can't write*"? (You know the answer to this one.)

**4.** Have I used euphemism to mask a stereotype? Is a wife "*a wonderful asset to her husband*" or something more in her own right?

# Editing for Grammar

An understanding of grammar will help you clarify how each word in your sentence contributes to the whole. It can also help you identify nonstandard language that may distract the reader from your meaning.

# 25   Eliminating Sentence Fragments

An English sentence expresses a complete idea; a sentence fragment does not. Fragments occur often in everyday speech; however, in academic writing, they are regarded as errors.

> None of us understood the result. <u>Or even how it had happened.</u>

You can eliminate sentence fragments in one of two ways: Either add the missing subject or verb (or both) to turn the fragment into a sentence, or incorporate the fragment into a nearby sentence.

## 25a.  Supplying verbs or subjects

To make a fragment a complete sentence, add the missing verb or subect.

> A fleet of colorful fishing boats *rocked* at anchor in the bay.
>
> The truck bounced off the guard rail. Then *it* careened across four lanes of traffic.

## 25b.  Joining fragments to sentences

A dependent clause has a subject and a verb, but it begins with a word such as *after, although, since, because, when, where,* or *whether.* These clauses cannot stand alone.

> This was devastating. ~~B~~*b*ecause the results had not been predicted.

## 25c.  Intentional fragments

In fiction, personal essays, and dialogue, writers occasionally use fragments to reproduce the sound of spoken language or for dramatic emphasis.

> *I knew that I was no legitimate resident in any world of ideas. I knew I couldn't think. All I knew then was what I couldn't do. All I knew then was*

*what I wasn't, and it took me some years to
discover what I was.*
<u>*Which was a writer.*</u>
<u>*By which I mean not a "good" writer or a
"bad" writer, but simply a writer, a person whose
most absorbed and passionate hours are spent arranging words on pieces of paper.*</u>

Joan Didion, "Why I Write" 127

If you want to use a fragment, think carefully about its effect and be sure it seems intentional. When your point war-
rants disrupting readers' expectations, consider using a
fragment. If it works.

## 26    Repairing Run-On Sentences

A run-on sentence consists of two complete sentences (independent clauses) that have been joined incorrectly. The
two most common mistakes are joining sentences with only
a comma—a **comma splice**—and joining two sentences
without using punctuation or without a conjunction—a
**fused sentence.**

Correctly joining two independent clauses to form one
sentence usually requires either a semicolon or a comma
and a coordinating conjunction. Use the technique that fits
the sentence.

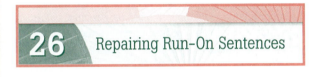

> Maya Angelou has worked as an actress and as a
> director, <sup>*but*</sup> her greatest success has come as a writer
> and poet.

> Top corporate executives can earn huge salaries;
> some are paid millions of dollars a year.

A semicolon is required when independent clauses
are joined with a coordinating conjunction such as *however*
or *therefore* or a transitional phrase like *for example.*

> The mayor presented her budget; however, the
> council had its own ideas.

## 26a.  Using a colon

Use a colon to join two independent clauses when the second clause explains, elaborates on, or illustrates the first.

It was not a perfect season; we lost one game.

## 26b.  Writing separate sentences

When one clause is much longer or different in structure, rewrite the two independent clauses as separate sentences.

My last year of high school was an eventful one and everything seemed to be happening all at once.

## 26c.  Using subordination

Place the less important idea in a dependent clause. Choose the subordinating conjunction (*after, as, because, before, if, than, that, when,* etc.) that best describes the relationship you want to establish.

The rain had frozen as it hit the ground, the streets were slippery.

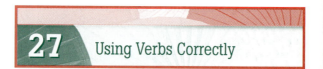

## 27   Using Verbs Correctly

Verbs convey action, but they can also provide other information, much of which is described in the accompanying chart. Always select the correct verb forms to convey the meaning you intend.

### Terms Used to Describe Verbs

**Person** indicates who or what performs an action: *I read, you read, he reads.*

**Number** indicates how many people or things perform the action: *she thinks, they think.*

**Tense** indicates the time of the action: *I learn, I learned, I will learn.*

**Mood** expresses the speaker's attitude toward or relation to the action: *You are quiet. Be quiet! I would be happier if you were quiet.*

**Voice** presents the subject as the (active) doer or (passive) receiver of the action: *She read the book. The book was read by her.*

# 27a.  Standard verb forms

Except for the verb *be,* all English verbs have five forms.

■ Two forms express **present action:**

Base form: I *act.*

*–s* form (*he, she, it*): He *acts.*

■ Three forms express **past action:**

**Past tense** (*-d, -ed* + base form): I *acted.*

**Past participle** (form of *be* or *have* + past participle): I *have acted.*

**Present participle** (*-ing* + base form) expresses continuing action (in present and past tense):

I am *acting.*

I was *acting.*

*Regular verbs* follow these patterns; *irregular verbs* form the past tense and past participle in other ways (see 27b).

## Using *-s* and *-ed* forms

Except for the verbs *be* and *have, –s* or *–es* is the ending for third-person singular regular verbs in the **present tense.**

The baby *sleeps.*

Everyone at the party *dances.*

Use standard verb forms in academic writing.

He ~~don't~~ doesn't need to study.

The **past tense** of all regular verbs is created by adding *-d* or *-ed* to the base form.

# 27b.  Irregular verb forms

Irregular verbs follow unpredictable patterns and thus are sometimes confusing. Some irregular verbs (including *bet, bid, burst, cost, cut, hit, hurt, quit, read, rid,* and *set*) do not change in any form:

I *hit* the ball now, but I *hit* it better yesterday. In the past, I have *hit* it even better.

Some others have a pattern of vowel changes:

I *ring* the bell today, and I *rang* it yesterday as I have *rung* it every morning.

*Be* is the most irregular verb.

| | |
|---|---|
| **Base form:** | be |
| **Present:** | am, are, is (*-s* form) |
| **Past:** | was, were |
| **Past participle:** | been |
| **Present participle:** | being |

Because the patterns of irregular verbs are not predictable, you may want to consult the following chart.

## Common Irregular Verbs

| BASE FORM | PAST TENSE (action completed) | PAST PARTICIPLE (action continues in present) |
|---|---|---|
| arise | arose | arisen |
| awake | awoke, awaked | awaked, awoken |
| be | was, were | been |
| bear | bore | borne, born |
| beat | beat | beaten, beat |
| become | became | become |
| begin | began | begun |
| bend | bent | bent |
| bind | bound | bound |
| bite | bit | bitten, bit |
| blow | blew | blown |
| break | broke | broken |
| bring | brought | brought |
| build | built | built |
| buy | bought | bought |
| catch | caught | caught |
| choose | chose | chosen |
| cling | clung | clung |
| come | came | come |
| creep | crept | crept |
| deal | dealt | dealt |
| dig | dug | dug |

*(continued)*

| | | |
|---|---|---|
| dive | dived, dove | dived |
| do | did | done |
| draw | drew | drawn |
| dream | dreamed, dreamt | dreamed, dreamt |
| drink | drank | drunk |
| drive | drove | driven |
| eat | ate | eaten |
| fall | fell | fallen |
| feed | fed | fed |
| feel | felt | felt |
| fight | fought | fought |
| find | found | found |
| flee | fled | fled |
| fly | flew | flown |
| forbid | forbade, forbad | forbidden |
| forget | forgot | forgotten, forgot |
| forgive | forgave | forgiven |
| freeze | froze | frozen |
| get | got | gotten, got |
| give | gave | given |
| go | went | gone |
| grow | grew | grown |
| hang (suspend) | hung | hung |
| hang (execute) | hanged | hanged |
| have | had | had |
| hear | heard | heard |
| hide | hid | hidden |
| hold | held | held |
| keep | kept | kept |
| know | knew | known |
| lay (put) | laid | laid |
| lead | led | led |
| leap | leapt, leaped | leapt, leaped |
| leave | left | left |
| lend | lent | lent |
| let (allow) | let | let |
| lie (recline) | lay | lain |
| light | lit, lighted | lit, lighted |
| lose | lost | lost |
| make | made | made |
| mean | meant | meant |
| meet | met | met |
| mistake | mistook | mistaken |

*(continued)*

| BASE FORM | PAST TENSE | PAST PARTICIPLE |
|-----------|------------|-----------------|
| pay | paid | paid |
| prove | proved | proved, proven |
| ride | rode | ridden |
| ring | rang | rung |
| rise | rose | risen |
| run | ran | run |
| say | said | said |
| see | saw | seen |
| seek | sought | sought |
| send | sent | sent |
| shake | shook | shaken |
| shoot | shot | shot |
| show | showed | shown, showed |
| shrink | shrank | shrunk |
| sing | sang | sung |
| sink | sank, sunk | sunk |
| sit | sat | sat |
| slay | slew | slain |
| sleep | slept | slept |
| speak | spoke | spoken |
| spin | spun | spun |
| spit | spit, spat | spit, spat |
| spring | sprang, sprung | sprung |
| stand | stood | stood |
| steal | stole | stolen |
| stick | stuck | stuck |
| sting | stung | stung |
| stink | stank, stunk | stunk |
| strike | struck | struck, stricken |
| swear | swore | sworn |
| swim | swam | swum |
| swing | swung | swung |
| take | took | taken |
| teach | taught | taught |
| tear | tore | torn |
| tell | told | told |
| think | thought | thought |
| throw | threw | thrown |
| wake | woke, waked | woken, waked, woke |
| wear | wore | worn |
| win | won | won |
| write | wrote | written |

# 27c. *Sit* and *set, lie* and *lay*

Because these pairs of words sound similar and are related in meaning, they are often confused. Here's how to tell them apart.

*Set* and *lay* mean "to place." They need an object to complete their meaning (what is being placed?).

direct object        direct object

I *set* the <u>table</u> each morning before I *lay* the <u>mail</u> on the desk.

*Sit* ("to be seated") and *lie* ("to recline") need no object to complete their meaning.

I will *sit* outside for a while, but soon I'll want to *lie* down.

*Lie* and *lay* get particularly confusing since the past tense of *lie* is *lay*! To use these correctly, first establish your meaning. Are you setting or laying something? Or are you just enjoying yourself sitting and lying down?

The books were just ~~laying~~ lying on the table.

She asked me to come in and ~~set~~ sit with her awhile.

# 27d. Auxiliary verbs

Main verbs often require **auxiliary** or **helping verbs,** commonly forms of *be, have,* or *do.* Together, the auxiliary verb and main verb form a **verb phrase.**

verb phrase<br>auxiliary    main verb

Tyler *has been working*.

Auxiliary verbs do various jobs in sentences:

The student council *is considering* what to do about it. *(present progressive tense)*

They *do want* to go to the conference. *(emphasis)*

*Has* he *received* the blueprints? *(question)*

He *does* not *intend* to leave without them. *(negative statement)*

The blueprints *were delivered* on Friday. *(passive voice)*

Forms of *have, do,* and *be* change form to indicate tense and number.

- *have, has, had*
- *do, does, did*
- *be, am, is, are, was, were, being, been*

I *have mended* a jacket that *had been* torn.

## Modal auxiliaries

*Can, could, may, might, must, shall, should, will,* and *would* are used with a main verb to express condition, intent, permission, possibility, obligation, or desire. These **modal auxiliaries** cannot serve as main verbs; they always appear with the base form of the verb. They do not change form.

Staying in touch with old friends *can be* difficult.

*Can* she *dance?* Yes, she *can.* (*dance is understood here*)

## Using auxiliary verbs correctly

Standard English requires the auxiliary verb *be* or *have* with present participles and past participles.

Gina $\overset{is}{\underset{\wedge}{}}$ running for student council.

She $\overset{has}{\underset{\wedge}{}}$ spoken to everyone about it.

A form of *be—is, are, was, were, has been—*along with the main verb is needed to create the passive voice.

Each student *is given* a book at graduation.

## Transitive and intransitive verbs

Some verbs require a direct object—a word or words that indicate who or what received the action of the verb.

direct object
They documented *their results.*

A verb that has a direct object is a ***transitive verb.*** A verb that does not have a direct object is an ***intransitive***

**verb.** Many verbs may be either transitive or intransitive, depending on the context.

> **Transitive:** Joey *grew* tomatoes last summer.

> **Intransitive:** The tomatoes *grew* rapidly.

## Linking verbs

**Linking verbs** include *be, become, appear, seem,* and other verbs describing existence, as well as verbs describing sensations—*look, feel, taste, smell, sound.* They link the subject of a sentence to an element that renames or identifies the subject. That element, a *subject complement,* can be a noun or an adjective.

A linking verb, like an equal sign, links two equivalent terms.

| | |
|---|---|
| Sue is nice. | Sue = nice |
| They felt tired. | They = tired |
| Jake was a recent graduate. | Jake = graduate |

## 27e.  Verb tense

English has three *simple* tenses, three *perfect* tenses, and a *progressive* form for each of them.

The three **simple tenses** indicate *present, past,* or *future* action. **Simple present** tense describes something occurring at same time of speaking.

> He *looks* happy today. He usually *looks* pretty content.

Simple present is also used to state general facts or truths and when writing about literature.

> In *The Tempest,* the wizard Prospero *seems* to control the heavens.

**Simple past** tense describes actions *completed in the past.*

> He *looked* a little depressed yesterday.

**Simple future** tense describes actions that *will occur in the future* or predictable events.

> He *will look* different tomorrow.

The three **perfect tenses** indicate *action completed by a specific time*. Using forms of *have* + the past participle, they place that action in the present, past, or future. **Present perfect** describes action completed in the past or a completed action still occurring.

> She *has looked* for the file today.

**Past perfect** describes action completed before another past action took place.

> She *had looked* for the file ten times before she found it.

**Future perfect** describes an action that will be completed at some specific time in the future.

> Once she goes through the last drawer, she *will have looked* everywhere.

The three **progressive tenses** describe *continuing action* in the present, past, or future. **Present progressive** describes ongoing action in the present.

> She *is anticipating* the holidays.

**Past progressive** describes continuous action in the past with no specified end.

> Before her father's illness, she *was anticipating* the holidays.

**Future progressive** expresses a continuous or ongoing action in the future that ordinarily depends on some other action or circumstance.

> Once her father is better, she *will be anticipating* the holidays again.

The three **perfect progressive** tenses describe action that continues up to a specific time of completion in the present, past, or future. **Present perfect progressive** describes action that began in the past and still continues.

> He *has been looking* for a job since August.

**Past perfect progressive** describes ongoing action that was completed before some other action.

> Before he found work, he *had been looking* for a job for six months.

**Future perfect progressive** describes continuous action that will be completed at some future time.

> By August, he *will have been looking* for a job for six months.

# 27f.   Sequence of tenses

Many combinations of verb tenses are possible in the same sentence. The *sequence of tenses* must describe events accurately and make sense.

> present                    future
> I think that you will enjoy this movie.
> *(I am thinking this before you go to the movie.)*

> present             present
> I know that you like foreign films.
> *(I am knowing this at the same time you are liking foreign films.)*

> present                  past
> I believe that you misunderstood me.
> *(I believe this after you misunderstood me.)*

## Sequences with infinitives and participles

The infinitive of a verb (*to* + base form) and the present and past participles have tenses as well. The tense of an infinitive or a participle must be in sequence with the tense of the main verb.

### Infinitives

Use *present infinitives* to show action occurring at same time as, or later than, the action of the main verb.

> Some children like to play with educational toys.

Use the *present perfect infinitive* to show action that occurred before the main verb.

> I seem to have misplaced my bank card.

### Present participles

Use *present participles* to show action occurring at same time as the action of the main verb.

> Working feverishly, he wrote late into the night.

Use the *present perfect participle* to show action completed before the action of the main verb.

<u>Having worked</u> feverishly all night, at dawn he <u>saw</u> the sunrise.

### Past participles

Use *past participles* to show action taking place at same time as or completed before the action of the main verb.

<u>Guided</u> by instinct, the birds <u>returned</u> as usual on March 19.

## 27g. Mood

English has three verb moods:

1. **Indicative** mood is used for facts, opinions, and questions.

   He *believes* the theory is valid.

2. **Imperative** mood is used for commands or directives.

   *Knead* the dough until it forms a ball.

3. **Subjunctive** mood expresses wishes, requirements, or conditions contrary to fact.

   If Benjamin Franklin *were* alive, he would marvel at his lasting fame.

## 27h. Voice

The *voice* of a verb tells you whether its subject is the actor **(active voice)** or the receiver of the action **(passive voice).** The active voice is simpler, more direct, and thus more quickly understood by the reader.

She *read* the book. *(active voice)*

The book *was read* by her. *(passive voice)*

For more on active versus passive voice, see 21d.

## 28    Subject-Verb Agreement

Verbs must agree with their subjects in number (Are you talking about one or more than one?) and person (Who is the featured person? I? You? She or he? It? They?). Matters of agreement often come down to the addition of the letter *s* in the third-person singular.

|  | SINGULAR | PLURAL |
|---|---|---|
| **First person:** | I think | we think |
| **Second person:** | you think | you think |
| **Third person:** | he/she/it thin*ks* | they think |

This works for many verbs in common usage. However, the verb *be* has very different forms in the present and past tenses:

| PRESENT TENSE | | PAST TENSE | |
|---|---|---|---|
| I am | we are | I was | we were |
| you are | you are | you were | you were |
| he/she/it is | they are | he/she/it was | they were |

Sometimes subject-verb agreement can be confusing. Consider the following issues when you're unsure.

## 28a. Interruptions between subject and verb

Sometimes words placed between the subject and verb can confuse the issue. To help you determine what verb is needed, eliminate the interrupting words and test for the proper match.

The bouquet of flowers ~~are~~ *is* very fragrant.

*(Translate sentence to The bouquet . . . is very fragrant. Singular subject, bouquet, takes singular verb, is.)*

Mr. Johnson, along with his children, ~~were~~ *was* waiting outside.

*(Translate sentence to Mr. Johnson . . . was waiting outside. Singular subject, Mr. Johnson, takes singular verb, was.)*

## 28b. Subjects linked by *and*

Two or more subjects linked by *and* (compound subjects) are almost always plural.

Peter and Patrick *play* on the lacrosse team.

***Exception:*** When the two joined words make up a single entity, it requires a singular verb.

Red beans and rice *is* my favorite dish.

## 28c.  Subjects joined by *or* or *nor*

Make the verb agree with the subject closer to it.

> Neither the researchers nor the professor *accepts* the results.
>
> **(Singular *professor* is closer to the verb; use a singular verb, *accepts*.)**
>
> Neither the professor nor the researchers *accept* the results.
>
> **(Plural *researchers* is closer to the verb; use a plural verb, *accept*.)**

# 28d.  Collective nouns

Words that refer to groups of people, animals, or things (*couple, flock, crowd, herd, committee*) are called *collective nouns.* Such words can take either singular or plural verbs, depending on whether you consider the group as a whole or a composite of individuals.

> The jury *has* reached a verdict.
>
> **(Here the group, *jury,* is considered as one unit and takes a singular verb, *has*.)**
>
> The jury *have* returned home.
>
> **(Here *jury* is considered a group of individuals and therefore takes a plural verb, *have*.)**

*Media, data, curricula, criteria,* and *phenomena* look like singular words in English but in fact are plural forms of words (from Greek and Latin sources) like *criterion* and *phenomenon* and should therefore take *plural* verbs:

> The media ~~has~~ *have* continued to focus on crime even as data ~~shows~~ *show* that cities are becoming safer.

# 28e.  Indefinite pronouns

Indefinite pronouns do not refer to *specific* persons or things. Pronouns such as *anybody, anyone, anything, each, either, everybody, everyone, everything, neither, no one, one, somebody, someone,* and *something* are considered singular and take singular verbs.

Someone *has* been sleeping in my bed.

Everybody *wears* a heavy coat in this weather.

Some other indefinite pronouns, such as *all, any,* and *some,* can be singular or plural.

All *are* required to take the exam.

All I have *is* a rough idea.

***Note:*** Although some controversy exists about the way it sounds, the word *none* takes a singular verb.

The birds all escaped, and none *was* recaptured.

## 28f. *Who, which,* and *that*

To match the verb to your pronoun, consider the word to which it refers.

<u>Barb and Robin</u>, who *want* to join the project, have applied.

(In this sentence, *who* refers to the plural *Barb and Robin* and therefore takes the plural verb *want.*)

A <u>bale</u> of shingles that *slips* off the roof could hurt someone.

(In this sentence, *that* refers to the singular *bale* and therefore takes the singular verb *slips.*)

## 28g. Nouns ending in *s*

*Statistics, politics, economics, athletics, measles, news, acoustics,* and *aesthetics* look like plural nouns but take singular verbs.

Economics *is* sometimes called "the dismal science."

***Exception:*** When these nouns refer to specific instances or characteristics, they are considered plural and take a plural verb.

The economics of the project *make* no sense.

## 28h. Titles used as words

Titles, even those that include plurals or words joined by *and,* are considered singular and take a singular verb.

"Shake, Rattle, and Roll" *was* recorded by Bill Haley and the Comets.

General Motors *is* an important employer in Michigan.

## 29    Pronouns

A pronoun is a stand-in for a noun: *she, it, them, me,* and so on. Problems with pronouns usually focus on one of three areas:

1. **Reference:** Is it clear to whom the pronoun refers?
2. **Agreement:** Does it agree with the noun to which it's linked?
3. **Case:** When do you use *I* or *me*? *Who* or *whom*?

## 29a.  Reference

The word to which a pronoun refers is called its *antecedent.* Problems occur when references are ambiguous or unclear.

### Ambiguous reference

An ambiguous sentence can be read in more than one way.

Marco met Roger as *he* arrived at the gym.

To whom does *he* refer, Marco or Roger? To make the meaning clear, revise the sentence.

As Marco arrived at the gym, he met Roger.

Marco met Roger as Roger arrived at the gym.

### Unclear reference

Interviews with several television newspeople made ~~it~~ reporting seem like a fascinating career.

*(Without being explicit here, the reader doesn't know what career seems fascinating.)*

## Vague reference by *this, that,* or *which*

When *this, that,* or *which* refers to a general idea, clarification may be needed. Explicitly stating the antecedent usually works.

> No one has suggested taxing health care.
> This $\overset{\text{tax}}{\underset{\wedge}{\text{is}}}$ unlikely.
>
> *(Without the added word, it's not clear whether the suggestion or the tax is unlikely.)*

## Vague reference with *it, they,* or *you*

Although these pronouns are often clear when people are speaking, academic writing requires explicit reference.

> $\overset{\text{According to}}{\cancel{\text{It said on}}}$ the news this morning $_\wedge$ ~~that~~ the game was canceled.
>
> $\overset{\text{The club doesn't}}{\underset{\wedge}{\cancel{\text{They don't}}}}$ let anyone in without a shirt or shoes.

# 29b. Pronoun–antecedent agreement

Personal pronouns should agree with their antecedents in number, person, and gender.

> Mrs. Shah held the door for *her* daughter.
>
> *(Singular pronoun her refers to Mrs. Shah.)*

> The Shahs were on *their* way to the antique show.
>
> *(Plural pronoun their refers to more than one Shah.)*

## Sexist pronouns

Agreement becomes a problem when pronouns refer to indefinite antecedents such as *anyone, someone,* and *everyone.* Because these pronouns can refer to either males or females, be careful in your use of pronouns. Consider the following:

> If anyone needs to miss class, he will need to contact the instructor.

This is not acceptable because *he* refers only to males and is considered sexist.

If anyone needs to miss class, they will need to contact the instructor.

This is acceptable in terms of gender but not in terms of grammar because the plural pronoun *they* does not agree with the singular antecedent *anyone*.

To address this problem, consider (1) using the phrase *he or she,* (2) revising the sentence using the plural noun *students* in place of *anyone,* or (3) eliminating personal pronouns altogether: *Students who miss class will need to contact the instructor.*

## Agreement with antecedents joined by *and*

Pronouns referring to a compound antecedent should be plural.

The book and the folders are in *their* places on the shelf.

## Agreement with antecedents joined by *or* and *nor*

Make your pronoun agree with the antecedent closest to it.

Either the equipment failures or the bad weather

will take *its* toll.

*(The singular pronoun its refers to the closest antecedent, weather, which is singular.)*

## Agreement with collective nouns

Use a singular pronoun to refer to collective nouns (*couple, flock, crowd*) that are seen as a single group or unit.

The flock rose suddenly from the pond and took up
*its*
~~their~~ usual formation.

Use a plural pronoun if members of the group act individually.

The couple *disagree* about the plan.

## Agreement with indefinite pronouns

Words like *anyone, everyone, someone, anybody, everybody, somebody, anything, everything, something, either, neither, each, nothing, much, one,* and *no one* do not refer to a specific person, place, or thing. They are always singular and should take a singular pronoun.

<u>Neither</u> of these books has *its* original cover.

<u>Someone</u> has lost *his* necktie.

In the second example, if the gender of the necktie loser is not clear, either write *Someone has lost his or her necktie* (pretty awkward) or change the construction to make it gender-neutral: *Someone has lost a necktie.*

The indefinite pronouns *few, many, both,* and *several* are always plural and therefore require a plural pronoun.

<u>Few</u> of the students have completed *their* work.

The indefinite pronouns *some, any, all, more, most,* and *none* can be singular or plural depending on their context.

In a survey of young voters, <u>some</u> said *they* were conservative.

<u>Some</u> of the gemstone has lost *its* luster.

## 29c. Pronoun case

Because pronouns are stand-ins for nouns, they perform different roles in sentences, just as nouns do. These different roles are called *cases*. Use the *subjective case* of a pronoun for the person or thing that performs the action in the sentence: <u>She</u> plays piano. Use the *objective case* when the pronoun receives the action: *Bob gave the book to <u>her</u>.* Use the *possessive case* to show ownership: *That book is <u>mine</u>.*

| SUBJECTIVE | OBJECTIVE | POSSESSIVE |
|---|---|---|
| I | me | my |
| you | you | your |
| he/she/it | him/her/it | his/her/its |
| we | us | our |
| you | you | your |
| they | them | their |

***Note:*** Use the possessive pronouns to precede a noun: *Megan is <u>her</u> sister.* However, use the following possessive pronouns when no noun follows: *mine, yours, his, hers, ours, theirs.*

### Compound subjects

Choosing the correct pronoun can be tricky when two or more words are joined. Test the sentence without the added words to determine the correct pronoun.

Todd and ~~me~~ *I* pruned the tall white pine.

*(When you test the sentence as* me pruned the tall white
pine, *it is clear the pronoun should be* I, *as in* I pruned the
tall pine.*)*

## Subject complements

Subject complements follow linking verbs and rename or
describe the subject (see 27d). Use the subjective case for
subject complements.

The winners were Gina and ~~me~~ *I*.

## Compound objects

Two or more objects joined by *and, or,* or *nor* are considered *compound objects.* Use the objective case for each
part of the construction.

Just between you and ~~I~~ *me*, it's a fake.

I spoke with Nancy and ~~they~~ *them* about the competition.

## Appositives

**Appositives** rename nouns or pronouns and must have
the same case as the words they rename.

It was the victors, Paul and *he,* who wanted to
leave.
*(The appositive* Paul and he *is in the subjective case.)*

They asked the teachers, Barbara and *me,* to help out.
*(The appositive* Barbara and me *is in the objective case.)*

## *We* or *us* before a noun

To determine which case to use, omit the noun and test for
appropriate use.

~~Us~~ *We* hikers were worried about the weather.

They told ~~we~~ *us* hikers not to worry.

## Pronoun case with verbals

Participles, gerunds, and infinitives are called *verbals* because they are derived from verbs. Each can have objects.

When a pronoun functions as the object of a verbal, use the objective case.

> **Participle:** I saw Robert greeting *him*.
>
> **Gerund:** Seeing *her* made the holiday complete.
>
> **Infinitive:** Robert was glad to see *her*.

## Pronouns before gerunds

Use the possessive case when a pronoun precedes a verbal (gerund) used as a noun.

> ~~Me~~ <sup>My</sup> leaving made them all sad.

## Pronouns before infinitives

Use the objective case for pronouns preceding infinitives.

> They want *her* to help.

## Case after *than* or *as*

When determining the correct choice of pronouns in these cases, it is helpful to fill in the missing words.

> She likes her dog better than _____ (me? I?).

Construct test sentences to see which you mean.

> She likes her dog better than I (like her dog).
>
> She likes her dog better than (she likes) me.

In the first sentence, use *I* as the subject of *like.* In the second, use *me* as the object of *likes.*

# 29d. *Who or whom*

The distinction between *who* and *whom* has all but disappeared from everyday speech, but in writing be careful to use *who* for subjects and *whom* for objects.

## In questions

To decide whether to use *who* or *whom* in a question, turn the question into a statement by substituting *he/she* or *him/her*. If *he/she* fits, use *who*. If *him/her* fits, use *whom*.

> *Who* had the authority to enter the building at night?
>
> *(She had the authority, so use* who.*)*

When a pronoun is the object of the verb or the object of the preposition, use *whom.*

To *whom* are you speaking?

*(You are speaking to* him, *so use* whom.*)*

## In dependent clauses

To choose between *who* or *whom* in a dependent clause, check for the word's function within the clause.

That woman, ~~who~~ *whom* I met last week, won the Nobel Prize for chemistry.

*(Whom is the object of the verb* met, *even though it re-names the subject of the main clause,* woman.*)*

She tells that same story to ~~whomever~~ *whoever* will listen.

*(Whoever is the subject of* will listen, *even though the en-tire subordinate clause* whoever will listen *is the object of the preposition* to.*)*

The *he/she, him/her* test for questions also works here.

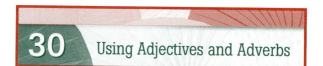

# 30  Using Adjectives and Adverbs

Adjectives and adverbs add information about other words in a sentence but differ in terms of the types of words they modify.

## 30a.  Adjective or adverb?

**Adjectives** modify (describe, identify, or limit) nouns or pronouns.

Hector is a *fine* father who has *gentle* hands and *abundant* patience with *crying* babies.

He is *loving, careful,* and *dependable.*

*Fine, gentle, abundant,* and *crying* are words that de-scribe the nouns to which they're attached: *father, hands, patience,* and *babies;* since they modify nouns, they're called *adjectives.* The words *loving, careful,* and *depen-dable* modify the pronoun *he* and are also adjectives.

**Adverbs** modify verbs, adjectives, other adverbs, and sometimes whole clauses.

> He *often* takes care of the baby at *truly* late hours and *nearly always* quiets her *quickly*.

When modifying verbs, adverbs tell when, where, how, why, and under what conditions something happens (how often, to what degree). *Often* and *always* modify verbs in this sentence. *Truly* modifies *late* (adjective); *nearly* modifies *always* (adverb).

## Suffixes

Adjectives are often formed by adding endings such as *–able*, *–ful*, and *–ish* to nouns and verbs: *acceptable, beautiful, foolish*. Adverbs are often formed by adding *–ly* to an adjective: *nearly, amazingly, brilliantly*. However, an *ly* ending does not always mean that a word is an adverb. A number of adjectives end in *ly: brotherly, early, friendly, lovely*. And many adverbs do not end in *ly: always, here*.

## 30b. Adjectives

Adjectives usually come before nouns, but they can also follow a linking verb such as *be, become, appear, grow*, and *seem* to describe the subject: *He seems sad*.

The linking verbs *appear, look, smell, taste*, and *sound* can also function as action verbs. If you are describing an action, use an adverb: *The ghost of Hamlet's father appears <u>suddenly</u>*.

## 30c. Adverbs

In casual speech, adjectives are sometimes used instead of adverbs to modify verbs: *It fit real well* instead of *It fit really well*. Be sure to use the correct forms of the following pairs.

### *Bad* and *badly*

Use *bad* only as an adjective with a linking verb (see 27d) and *badly* as an adverb with other verbs.

> She looked as though she felt ~~badly~~ <sup>bad</sup>.

> They were playing so ~~bad~~ <sup>badly</sup> that I left at halftime.

## *Good* and *well*

*Good* is always an adjective; *well* can be either an adjective meaning "healthy" or an adverb meaning "skillfully."

She sings ~~good~~ *well* enough to get the lead.

The hat looked ~~well~~ *good* on my mother.

## *Less* and *fewer*

*Less* and *fewer* are both adjectives, but they function in different ways. *Less* describes something considered as a whole unit: *less hope, less money. Fewer* describes quantities that can be counted: *fewer hopes, fewer dollars.*

The house would lose <u>less</u> heat if ~~less~~ *fewer* windows were open.

# 30d.   Comparatives and superlatives

Adjectives and adverbs have three forms: the *positive,* the *comparative,* and the *superlative.* The positive form of an adjective or adverb describes a particular property (*smart, funny*); the comparative compares that property between *two* people or things (*smarter, funnier*); and the superlative makes a comparison among *three or more* people or things (*smartest, funniest*). Some lengthy adjectives and most adverbs ending in *ly* take *more* and *most* to form comparative and superlative forms. Negative comparisons are formed by using *less* and *least.*

| POSITIVE | COMPARATIVE | SUPERLATIVE |
|---|---|---|
| big | bigger | biggest |
| fast | faster | fastest |
| good | better | best |
| careful | more careful | most careful |
| hopeful | less hopeful | least hopeful |

Which modifier you choose can tell a lot about what you're comparing.

Of the brothers, Joe was the *stronger* athlete.

*(There are two brothers.)*

Of the brothers, Joe was the *strongest* athlete.

*(There are at least three brothers.)*

Do not use double comparatives or superlatives. When forming comparatives, use either *–er* or *more,* not both. When forming superlatives, use either *–est* or *most,* not both.

After eating, he felt ~~more~~ better.

## 30e.  Avoiding double negatives

In English, one negative modifier (*no, not, never*) is sufficient to change the meaning of a sentence. When two negatives appear in the same sentence, they cancel each other out: *I didn't have no money* literally means *I had some money.* Eliminate double negatives.

# 31  Positioning Modifiers

In English, word order is critical to meaning. It makes a difference whether you say *The man ate the fish* or *The fish ate the man.*

## 31a.  Misplaced modifiers

Modifiers should point clearly to the words they modify. As a rule, related words should be kept together. A misplaced modifier can modify other words than the one the writer intended: *We wanted our ordeal to end desperately.*

Unless this writer wanted things to turn out badly, the modifier is misplaced. Put the adverb (*desperately*) before the verb (*wanted*) in order to clarify the sentence: *We desperately wanted our ordeal to end.*

### Limiting modifiers

Put adverbs such as *almost, even, hardly, just, merely, nearly, only, scarcely,* or *simply* directly before the words you want them to modify.

We want *only* her to sing a song. *(no one else)*
We want her to sing only one song. *(no more than that)*
*Only* we want her to sing. *(No one else does.)*

## 31b.  Dangling modifiers

A modifier needs to be adjacent to the word it modifies; otherwise confusion can result. A modifier is said to "dangle" when the element it is supposed to modify is missing.

Dangling modifiers most often appear at the beginning of sentences in which a subject (actor) is not specified.

> Running through the rain, our clothes were soaked.

This sentence suggests that *our clothes* were running through the rain. The actor of the sentence—*we*—is missing. To correct a dangling modifier, place the modified element directly after the modifier, and supply a new verb if necessary.

> Running through the rain, ~~our~~ *we got* clothes ~~were~~ soaked.

## 31c.  Split infinitives

An infinitive consists of *to* plus a verb: *to fly, to grow, to achieve.* When a modifier comes between its two parts, an infinitive is "split": *to quickly speak.* Split infinitives occur in speech, but they are considered awkward in writing.

> She needed to ~~carefully~~ make the decision. *carefully*

Sometimes, however, a split infinitive is the least awkward choice.

> She vowed to *better* serve all parts of the community.

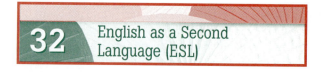

| **32** | English as a Second Language (ESL) |

This chapter is designed to provide help with the most common problems in writing encountered by students who are learning English as a second language.

## 32a.  Articles

The articles *the, a,* and *an* are used to introduce nouns. *A* and *an* are called *indefinite articles.* Use them with words not fully specified or identified. *The* is called the *definite* article. Use it with nouns already mentioned or specified.

> I had *a* dream. *The* dream seemed very real.

*(The dream refers back to the one just specified.)*

# When to use *a* or *an*

Use *a* or *an* with singular words that name persons, places, or things that can be counted (*count nouns*): *one bird, two birds; one chair, two chairs.*

> She bought *a* car by reading *an* advertisement in the paper.

> Use *a* before a consonant sound: *a bowl, a happy person.* Use *an* before a vowel sound: *an insect, an honest person.*

# When not to use *a* or *an*

Do not use *a* or *an* with nouns that refer to things or abstractions that cannot be counted (*noncount nouns*): *water, oil, sand, money.*

> The boys brought *sand* back from the beach.

> If you want to express a specific amount—an amount that can be counted—add a quantifier in front of the noncount noun: *a stick of butter, a gallon of water.*

### Common Noncount Nouns

Names of food and drink: *bacon, fish, milk, tea*

Nonfood substances: *air, coal, dirt, paper*

Areas of study: *art, biology, economics, history*

Ideas and emotions: *anger, beauty, health, love*

Other: *clothing, equipment, furniture, homework, jewelry*

# When to use *the*

Use the definite article *the* with singular count nouns or noncount nouns in the following cases.

1. The noun has already been mentioned.

   There is *a problem* with this approach.
   *The problem* is a subtle one.

   The boys brought *sand* for the garden.
   They got *the sand* from the beach.

2. The noun is made specific by modifiers.

   *The man in the blue suit* is the mayor.

   *(The phrase* in the blue suit *identifies the specific man.)*

**3.** The context makes the noun's identity clear.

Please open *the window.*

*(Both the speaker and the listener know which window is meant.)*

## When not to use *the*

Do not use *the* with plural or noncount nouns used in the sense of "all" or "in general."

~~The m~~ilk is an important source of calcium.

*(M with caret above, replacing "The m")*

Do not use *the* with most singular proper nouns: names of people (*Abraham Lincoln*); names of streets, parks, cities, and states (*Union Street, Glacier National Park, Boston, Maine*); names of continents and most countries (*Asia, Peru*); and names of bays and single lakes, mountains, and islands (*Penobscot Bay, Lake Superior, Mount Washington, Bermuda*).

Exceptions include geographic features and regions (*the West Coast, the Sahara, the Yucatan peninsula, the Atlantic Ocean, the Black Sea, the Gulf of Mexico, the Panama Canal, the Ohio River*).

*Note:* *The* is used to mark plural proper nouns: *the United States, the Great Lakes, the Green Mountains, the Bahamas.*

## 32b.  Prepositions

A preposition shows a relationship between ideas or objects in a sentence. The relationships can be in space, time, or manner.

### SPACE
The television set is *on* the table.

### TIME
Let's have popcorn *after* the movie.

### MANNER
John eats his popcorn *with* butter.

Prepositions can pose a challenge for nonnative speakers of English because many prepositions can have more than one meaning. (*I left <u>at</u> noon. I threw the ball <u>at</u> the wall.*) When you're unsure which preposition to use, ask a native speaker or check a dictionary.

## 32c. Phrasal verbs

*Phrasal verbs* consist of a verb and a particle, similar to a preposition, that alters the verb's meaning. The changed meanings sometimes seem to make little sense, so study these verbs as you come across them.

| VERB | MEANING |
|---|---|
| bring up | raise (a person, a topic) |
| build up | make stronger |
| call off | cancel |
| catch up (with) | meet someone at a prearranged place *or* exchange news and/or gossip |
| check out | do research *or* appraise someone's looks |
| come up with | invent |
| cut down | reduce |
| figure out | discover, determine |
| find out | discover |
| get away | escape |
| get back | receive in return |
| get in | arrive *or* enter |
| get out | leave |
| get over | recover from |
| get rid of | eliminate, discard |
| get up | arise *or* stand |
| give up | quit, stop |
| go up and down | fluctuate |
| gone up | increased |
| grow up | become an adult |
| help out | assist |
| keep up | continue *or* stay abreast |
| let down | disappoint *or* break a promise |
| look into | investigate |
| look up | find (a phone number) *or* contact someone (to arrange a visit) |
| make up | invent *or* apologize after a fight *or* offer compensation |
| pick up | get, collect *or* meet someone at a party or bar |
| point out | tell *or* inform |
| run out | come to the end |
| set up | establish |
| settle down | relax *or* establish a permanent home |
| show off | look for attention or admiration |

| show up | appear |
| sign up | register (for a course, etc.) |
| slow down | relax *or* move more slowly |
| take off | depart *or* make free time |
| try out | test *or* audition (for a role in a play) |
| turn down | refuse a suggestion or an invitation *or* decrease the sound volume |
| turn off | disgust *or* stop |
| turn on | attract *or* arouse someone |
| turn up | increase the sound volume *or* visit unexpectedly |
| work out | exercise *or* solve a problem |

## 32d.  Adjectives

Adjectives describe nouns. They are most often placed before the nouns they describe. Although the order of adjectives before nouns is flexible, some types of adjectives usually occur before others. For example, an adjective describing size occurs before one describing color: *the large white house* rather than *the white large house*.

The following list shows the typical order of adjectives before nouns. Generally, avoid long strings of adjectives.

1. Determiner (of number or possession): *a, the, her, Bob's, that, these*
2. Order: *first, next, third*
3. Evaluation: *good, pretty, happy, interesting*
4. Size: *big, small, minuscule*
5. Shape: *oblong, squarish, round*
6. Condition: *broken, shiny*
7. Age: *old, young, new*
8. Color: *blue, green, magenta*
9. Material: *wooden, cotton*
10. Noun used as adjective: *flower* (as before *garden*)

1    2    6    7    10

One never forgets that first, shiny new sports car.

1    4    5    9

A few large square wooden boxes were stacked on the floor.

# Editing for Punctuation

The more carefully you punctuate, the more easily readers will understand you. Commas, semicolons, dashes, parentheses, and other punctuation marks show your audience where to pause and for how long as well as what to emphasize or consider a question, digression, or quotation. Misusing any of these sentence signals can cause confusion, misunderstanding, or loss of meaning.

# 33 End Punctuation

## 33a. Periods

Use a period at the end of a statement, a mild command, or a polite request.

Use a period, not a question mark, after an indirect question (a question that is reported but not asked directly).

I wonder who made the decision.

Use a single period to end the sentence when an abbreviation containing a period falls at the end of a sentence.

Her flight leaves at 6:15 a.m.

Use a period in abbreviations that end in lowercase letters.

Mr.   Mrs.   Ms.   in.   ft.   etc.   e.g.   i.e.   vs.

Dr.   Rev.   Msgr.   Mon.   Atty.   Gov.   Sen.

Jan.   St.   Ave.   p.   para.   fig.   vol.   a.m.   p.m.

Do not use periods in other abbreviations unless they stand for personal names.

US   UK   BC   AD   BA   PhD   MD

Do not use periods with acronyms, which are abbreviations formed from the first letter of a series of words to simplify the names of government agencies, corporations, and other entities.

NASA   NATO   AIDS   CNN   SAT   FBI   CIA
EPA   IRS   IRA   NCAA   IBM   RSVP   mph   rpm

## 33b. Question marks

Use a question mark at the end of a direct question. Direct questions are usually signaled by one of the reporter's question words—*who, what, where, when, why, how* (see Chapter 10)—or by inverted word order, with the verb before the subject.

Where is Times Square? How can I get there?

Use a question mark or a period at the end of a polite request. A question mark emphasizes politeness.

Would you please sit down?

Use a question mark when a sentence ends with a *tag question*—one that is added at the end—even though the independent clause is declarative.

This train goes to Times Square, doesn't it?

Use a question mark for a direct question in quotation marks. Put the question mark before the closing quotation mark, and use no other end punctuation. (See also 38e.)

"Have we missed the train?" she asked.

Use a question mark after each question in a series of questions, even if they are not all complete sentences. (Capitalization is optional, but be consistent.)

Where did Mario go? To the library? To the cafeteria? To class?

Use a question mark after a direct question set off by dashes.

When the phone rang—was it 7 a.m. already?— I jumped out of bed.

## 33c.  Exclamation points

Use an exclamation point to convey emphasis and strong emotion in sentences that are exclamations, strong commands, or interjections.

Wow! It's late! Stop the train!

In a direct quotation, place the exclamation point before the closing quotation mark, and do not use any other end punctuation. (See also 38e.)

"Ouch!" my brother cried. "That hurts!"

Use an exclamation point after an exclamation set off by dashes.

They told me—I couldn't believe it!—that I'd won.

Use exclamation points sparingly in college writing.

# 34 | Commas

Commas are the most frequently used punctuation mark in English because they help signal the many different ways in which sentences are divided into parts and how those parts are related.

## 34a. Commas that connect sentences

Use a comma before two or more sentences (independent clauses) when they are joined by words such as *for, and, nor, but, or, yet,* or *so* (coordinating conjunctions) in a compound sentence. (See also Chapter 26.)

> We must act quickly, or the problem will get worse.
>
> The farmers ate lunch at 10 a.m., and they rested in the shade.

The comma before the conjunction may be omitted when the two sentences are very short and closely related.

> The sun rose and the fog lifted.

## 34b. Commas after introductory elements

When a sentence begins with an element other than the subject (and its modifiers), put a comma after that introductory element.

> When Elizabeth I assumed the throne of England in 1558, the country was in turmoil.
>
> As a matter of fact, John knows the answer.
>
> His dream of glory destroyed, the boxer died an embittered man.
>
> Yes, we need to improve our parks.
>
> Angered, the bull charged once more.

However, the comma is optional when the introductory element is brief and confusion is unlikely.

> In 1963 an assassin's bullet shocked the world.

## 34c. Commas to set off supplementary information

A pause is in order when you include information in a sentence that is not essential to its meaning. That is, if you subtracted this nonrestrictive element, the sentence would still make perfect sense.

> Bus drivers, who are generally underpaid, work
> long hours at straight pay.

However, do not use commas when the information is essential to the meaning of the sentence.

> Students who are late will be prohibited from
> taking the exam.

If you are not sure if a modifier is essential to meaning, rewrite the sentence, leaving out the modifier. If the meaning does not change, the modifier is not essential.

Clauses that begin with *where, which, who, whom,* or *whose* (adjective clauses) can be either restrictive or nonrestrictive. *That* is used only in restrictive clauses. *Which* is used for both nonrestrictive and restrictive clauses.

### RESTRICTIVE (NECESSARY)

The team that scores the most points will receive a trophy.

### NONRESTRICTIVE (NOT NECESSARY)

The dinner party, which had been carefully planned, went smoothly.

## 34d. Commas between items in a series

A series consists of three or more words, phrases, or clauses that are equal in importance and grammatical form. The conjunction *and* or *or* usually precedes the final element.

Use a comma after each element in a series, including the one that precedes the conjunction.

### WORDS

He studied all the notes, memos, and reports.

### PHRASES

To accelerate smoothly, to stop without jerking, and to make correct turns requires skill.

## 34e.  Commas to separate equal modifiers

Commas separate two or more adjectives of equal weight that modify the same noun—*a warm, sunny day*. To test, try inserting *and* between them or reversing their order. If the resulting sentence still makes sense, you need a comma. (See also 32d.)

### COMMA REQUIRED

He put on a clean, pressed shirt.

He put on a pressed, clean shirt.

### NO COMMA USED

I found five copper coins.

## 34f.  Commas to set off parenthetical elements

A parenthetical element is a word, phrase, or clause that interrupts a sentence but does not affect its meaning. It may appear anywhere in the sentence and can be moved from one place to another without changing the meaning.

Use commas to set off parenthetical elements.

Surprisingly enough, none of the bicycles was stolen.

None of the bicycles, surprisingly enough, was stolen.

None of the bicycles was stolen, surprisingly enough.

## 34g.  Commas to set off contrast elements, tag sentences, and direct address

Jeremiah was a bullfrog, not a toad.

You received my application in time, I hope.

Lilith, I hope you are well.

## 34h.  Commas with quotations

Use commas to set off words that attribute direct quotations. The comma appears inside the quotation marks.

"When I went to kindergarten and had to speak English for the first time," writes Maxine Hong Kingston, "I became silent."

Use a question mark or an exclamation point alone, without any comma, at the end of a quoted question or exclamation.

"What does the latest survey show?" Marion asked.

Do not use commas when a quotation is preceded by *that* or when the quotation is worked naturally into the sentence.

He closed by saying that "time will prove us right."

The author wonders whether "time will prove us right."

## 34i.  Commas with numbers, dates, names, and places

Counting from the right, use a comma after every three digits in numbers with four or more digits.

2,700    79,087    467,391

Do not use a comma in page numbers, street numbers, ZIP codes, or years.

21001 Southern Boulevard    3300 BC

Use commas before and after the year when a date giving month, day, and year is part of a sentence.

Louis Armstrong was born on July 4, 1900, in New Orleans.

When only the month and year are given or when the day precedes the month, do not use a comma.

The war broke out in August 1914 and ended on 11 November 1918.

Commas set off a title or abbreviation following a name.

Joyce B. Wong, MD, supervised the CPR training.

Set off a state name with commas, when it follows the name of a city.

She was born in Dayton, Ohio, and retired to Tampa, Florida.

Commas separate each element of a full address given in a sentence. The ZIP code does not have a comma before it.

Please note that my address will be 169 Elm Street, Apartment 4, Boston, MA 02116.

## 34j.   Commas to prevent misreading

Even when no specific rule requires one, a comma is sometimes added to prevent misreading.

We will all pitch in, in the event of a problem.

Revising the sentence is often a better solution.

In the event of a problem, we will all pitch in.

# 35   Semicolons

Semicolons help in two ways: First, they join one closely related sentence to another; second, they can substitute for commas in a series. Semicolons are more common in academic writing than in informal writing.

## 35a.  Semicolons between sentences

Use a semicolon to join two closely related sentences, especially when the thought following the first sentence qualifies or contradicts it; in such cases, a semicolon substitutes for a period.

It rained in August; the leaves turned bright red in September.

Most dogs aim to please their owners; cats don't behave that way.

A semicolon may also be used with a coordinating conjunction (*and, but, or, for, nor, yet, so*) to join complex clauses, particularly when one or both of the clauses contain commas.

If the weather clears, we'll leave at dawn; and if it doesn't, given the dangerous trail conditions, we'll pack up and go home.

## 35b. Semicolons between items in a series

Use semicolons between elements in a series when at least one element of the series includes a comma.

> The candidates for the award are Darnell, who won the essay competition; Elaine, the top debater; and Kiesha, the theater director.

# 36    Colons

A colon is a more forceful stop within a sentence than a semicolon. As a mark of introduction, a colon alerts the reader that the information following it will provide further explanation. The colon also has specialized uses, as explained here.

## 36a. Colons as marks of introduction

Use a colon to introduce an explanation, example, list, or quotation. What precedes the colon must be a full sentence (independent clause). The explanation or example can be a single word, a phrase, or a clause.

> He has but one objective: success.

> He has three objectives: fame, money, and power.

A colon may be used in place of a period or semicolon to imply that one sentence helps make sense of the other.

> The budget agreement erected a wall between the mayor and the council: The mayor operated the city, but the council controlled the money.

Some writers capitalize the first word of a sentence that follows a colon, as in this book, and others prefer lowercase (see 41d).

When a full sentence precedes a quotation, use a colon.

> The song from *South Pacific* puts it well: "You've got to be carefully taught."

Use a colon to introduce a long quotation set off from the main text in block format (see Chapters 54 and 59).

## 36b.  Other uses of colons

Colons are used between divisions of time, biblical chapters and verses, and titles and subtitles as well as in business communication.

### Hours, minutes, and seconds

Court convened promptly at 9:00 a.m.

The official elapsed time for the race was 2:45:56.

### Biblical citations

Isaiah 14:10

In MLA style, use a period.

Isaiah 14.10

### Main titles and subtitles

*Blue Highways: A Journey into America*

"A Deep Darkness: A Review of *Out of Africa*"

### Salutations and memo headings

Dear Mr. Nader:

To: Alex Di Giovanni

From: Paul Nkwami

Subject: 2007 budget

# 37    Apostrophes

The apostrophe marks the possessive form of a noun or pronoun, helps form certain plurals, and indicates where a letter has been dropped in contractions.

## 37a.  Apostrophes to show possession or ownership

To form the possessive case, add either an apostrophe and *s* or just an apostrophe to nouns and certain indefinite pronouns.

## Singular nouns

Use an apostrophe and *s* to form the possessive of any noun that does not end in *s*.

> Brad Pitt's new movie is his best yet.

> Use an apostrophe and *s* to form the possessive of a singular noun ending in *s*. (If pronouncing the additional syllable is awkward, you may use the apostrophe alone.)

> Don't waste the class's time.

> The company produced Yeats' cycle of plays.

## Plural nouns

Use an apostrophe alone to form the possessive case of a plural noun ending in *s*.

> Some schools let boys play girls' sports.

## Compound nouns

To form the possessive of a compound noun, use an apostrophe and *s* on only the last word.

> He borrowed his mother-in-law's car.

> The secretary of state's office certified the results.

When nouns joined by *and* are individuals with separate possession, add an apostrophe and *s* to each noun.

> The documentary compared Aretha Franklin's and
> Diana Ross's early careers.

## Possessive apostrophes with indefinite pronouns

Use an apostrophe to show possession with certain indefinite pronouns, including *someone, anybody, no one, one,* and *another*.

> Someone's umbrella was left at the bank.

> It's no one's business but my own.

> Do not use an apostrophe and *s* with the indefinite pronouns *all, any, both, each, few, many, most, much, none, several, some,* and *such*. Use the preposition *of* to show possession with these pronouns, or use a pronoun that has a possessive form.

> Let's read the works of both.

# 37b. Apostrophes to form plurals of letters and words used as words

Use an apostrophe and *s* to form the plural of a word discussed as a word or term and to form the plural of letters.

> There are two *perhaps*'s in that sentence.

> The word *occurrence* is spelled with two *r*'s.

Note that words and letters referred to as themselves are italicized. The apostrophe and the final *s* are not italicized.

Use *s* without an apostrophe to form the plural of numbers and symbols.

> Some children have difficulty learning to write 8s.

> Avoid using &s and #s in your research papers.

# 37c. Apostrophes to form contractions

A contraction is a word in which one or more letters are intentionally omitted and replaced by an apostrophe.

> didn't     we're     they're     'bye

**COMMON CONTRACTIONS**

| | | | |
|---|---|---|---|
| cannot | can't | does not | doesn't |
| do not | don't | would not | wouldn't |
| has not | hasn't | have not | haven't |
| will not | won't | was not | wasn't |
| she would | she'd | it is | it's |
| who is | who's | you are | you're |
| I am | I'm | they are | they're |
| let us | let's | we have | we've |
| there is | there's | she is | she's |

An apostrophe can also be used to show that digits have been dropped from a number, especially a year or a decade.

> the class of '02     the '60s

# 38     Quotation Marks

Quotation marks indicate that you are using the exact words spoken or written by someone else. They also distinguish certain titles, foreign expressions, and special terms from the main body of the text. American English uses double quotation marks (" ") for quotations, titles, and so on, and single quotation marks (' ')—apostrophes on the typewriter and on many computers—for quotations within quotations (or titles within titles).

In quoting another person's exact words, you must enclose those words in quotation marks and indicate your source of information when appropriate.

Quotation style varies somewhat from discipline to discipline. This chapter follows the conventions of the Modern Language Association, the authority for papers written in the languages and literature. (See also Chapters 53-57.)

## 38a.  Quotation marks for direct quotations

When quoting another person's exact words directly, keep in mind the following two conventions.

Use quotation marks to enclose brief direct quotations of up to four typed lines of prose or up to three lines of poetry. Any parenthetical citation of a source goes after the closing quotation marks but before the period.

> In <u>Lives under Siege</u>, Ratzenburger argues that "most adolescents are far too worried about the next six months and far too unconcerned about the next sixty years" (84).

Use single quotation marks for a quotation within a quotation.

> After the election, the incumbent said, "My opponent will soon learn, as someone once said, 'You can't fool all of the people all of the time.'"

Longer quotations should be presented in block format without quotation marks (see 36a and Chapters 54 and 59).

## 38b.  Quotation marks for dialogue

Use quotation marks to set off dialogue. Using a new paragraph every time the speaker changes indicates who is speaking even without attributory words.

> "Early parole is not the solution to overcrowding," the prosecutor said. "We need a new jail."
>
> The chairman of the county commission asked, "How do you propose we pay for it?"
>
> "Increase taxes if you must, but act quickly."

If one speaker's words continue for more than a single paragraph, use quotation marks at the beginning of each new paragraph but at the end of only the last paragraph.

## 38c.  Quotation marks for certain titles

Use quotation marks for the titles of brief poems, book chapters and parts, magazine and journal articles, episodes of television series, and songs. (Use italics or underlining for titles of longer works, such as books, magazines and journals, recordings, films, plays, and television series.)

"Araby" is the third story in James Joyce's book *Dubliners*.

This chart appeared with the article "Will Your Telephone Last?" in November's *Consumer Reports*.

In my favorite episode of *I Love Lucy*, "Job Switching," Lucy and Ethel work in a chocolate factory.

Do *not* use quotation marks or italics for the following:

- Titles of parts of a work or series that are generic rather than specific:

  Chapter 6    Part II    Episode 43

- Titles of sacred works, parts of sacred works, and ancient manuscripts:

  the Talmud    the Bible    the Koran

■ Documents:

> the Constitution      the Gettysburg Address

# 38d.  Quotation marks for special purposes

## Translations

Use quotation marks around the translation of a foreign word or phrase into English. The foreign word or phrase itself is italicized.

> I've always called Antonio *fratellino,* or "little brother," because he is six years younger than I.

## Special terms

Use quotation marks (or italics) for specialized terms when they are first introduced.

> He called the new vegetable "broccoflower," a yellow-green cross between broccoli and cauliflower.

# 38e.  Quotation marks with other punctuation

Which punctuation mark comes first when a word is followed by a quotation mark and another mark of punctuation? Both logic and convention govern the order.

## Periods and commas

Put periods and commas inside closing quotation marks.

> After Gina read "The Erlking," Joe recited "Gunga Din."

## Colons and semicolons

Put colons and semicolons outside closing quotation marks.

> The sign read "Closed": there would be no soda today.

## Question marks, exclamation points, and dashes

Put question marks, exclamation points, and dashes inside closing quotation marks if they are part of the quotation and outside closing quotation marks if they are not.

> She asked, "Have you read 'The Tiger'?"

> I can't believe you've never read "The Lottery"!

> Emma's first word—"dada"—caused Tom to beam.

# 39     Other Punctuation Marks

## 39a.  Parentheses

Enclose elements in parentheses that would otherwise interrupt a sentence: explanations, examples, asides, and supplementary information.

Enclose explanations, examples, and asides within a sentence.

> Relatives of famous people who are now famous themselves include Angelica Huston (daughter of John) and Michael Douglas (son of Kirk).

Enclose the translation of a specialized term or foreign word that appears in italics.

> English also borrowed the Dutch word *koekje* ("cookie").

Set off the date of an event or the dates of a person's birth and death.

> The *Oxford English Dictionary* was first published under the editorship of James A. H. Murray (1888–1933).

Enclose cross-references to other parts of your paper or enclose documentation.

> (For more on documentation, see Chapters 47–49.)

> The map (p. 4) shows the areas of heaviest rainfall.

Enclose numbers or letters that introduce items in a list within a sentence.

> The dictionary provides (1) pronunciation, (2) etymology, (3) past meanings, and (4) usage citations for almost 300,000 words.

Do not place a comma directly before a set of parentheses.

> His favorite American author is Emily Dickinson (he refers to her as "my favorite recluse").

When a parenthetical sentence is not enclosed within another sentence, capitalize the first word and use end punctuation inside the final parenthesis.

> The countess of Dia is almost forgotten today. (She was quite well known in her own time.)

When a parenthetical sentence falls within another sentence, use no period, and do not capitalize the first word.

> Uncle Henry (he is my mother's brother) has won many awards for his charitable work.

# 39b. Dashes

Dashes set off explanations, definitions, examples, appositives, and other supplementary information. Set dashes without spaces on either side.

> The *frijoles refritos*—a Mexican specialty of refried beans—were homemade.
> We did not notice the rain—it began so softly.

Dashes emphasize contrasts.

> I haven't read many novels by European writers—not to mention those by Asian or African writers.

Dashes indicate a pause, interruption, or abrupt shift in thought.

> "Well, I guess I was a little late—OK, an hour late."
> "It's exciting to see an eagle—there's one now!"

## Dashes with other punctuation

Do not capitalize the first word set off by dashes within another sentence. If the set-off sentence is a question or an exclamation, use a question mark or an exclamation point at the end, but do not capitalize the first word.

> Ward and June Cleaver—who can forget their orderly world?—never once questioned their roles in life.

Do not use commas or periods immediately before or after a dash.

## Choices: commas, parentheses, or dashes?

Commas, parentheses, and dashes can all be used to set off nonessential material within a sentence. Use commas when the material being set off is closely related in meaning to the rest of the sentence.

> A dusty plow, the kind the early Amish settlers used, hung on the wall of the old barn.

Use parentheses when the set-off material is not closely related to the main sentence and you want to de-emphasize it.

> Two young boys found an old plow (perhaps as old as the first Amish settlement) hidden in the barn.

Use dashes when the set-off material is not closely related to the main sentence and you want to emphasize it.

> The old plow—the one his great-grandfather had used—was still in good working order.

Dashes are especially flexible punctuation marks, capable of substituting for periods and semicolons as well as commas and parentheses in fast, informal writing. But because speed and informality are sometimes frowned on in academic writing, use dashes judiciously.

## 39c.   Ellipsis points

Ellipsis points are three periods each preceded and followed by a space. They are used to mark the deliberate omission of words or sentences from direct quotations.

Use ellipsis points to indicate an omission within a sentence.

> In *Drawing on the Right Side of the Brain*, Betty
> Edwards tells the reader, "You may feel that . . . it's
> the drawing that is hard."

If the omission comes at the end of a sentence, use a period or other end punctuation before the ellipsis.

> Edwards says, "Drawing is not really very hard. . . .
> You may not believe me at this moment."

Use a whole line of spaced ellipsis points when you omit a line or more of poetry.

> She walks in beauty, like the night
> . . . . . . . . . . . . . . . . . . . . . . . . . . . . . .
> And all that's best of dark and bright
> Meet in her aspect and her eyes.

Use ellipsis points to indicate a pause or interruption in dialogue.

> "The panther tracks come from that direction, . . . but
> where do they go after that?" he wondered.

# 39d.  Brackets

Brackets enclose words that are added to or changed within direct quotations.

Brackets mark small changes that clarify the meaning of a reference or of a word or make quoted words read correctly within the context of a sentence.

> E. B. White writes, "Any noon in Madison Square,
> you may see [a sparrow] pick up a straw in his beak,
> [and] put on an air of great business, twisting his
> head and glancing at the sky."

Use the Latin word *sic* ("such") within brackets to indicate that an error in quoted material was present in the original.

> In its statement, the commission said that its new
> health insurance program "will not effect [sic] the
> quality of medical care for county employees."

Within parentheses, use brackets to avoid double parentheses.

Theodore Bernstein explains that a person who feels sick is *nauseated:* "A person who feels sick is not *nauseous* any more than a person who has been poisoned is *poisonous.*" ("Dos, Don'ts, and Maybes of English Usage" [New York: Times Books, 1977]).

## 39e.  Slashes

The slash (/) is a slanted line to separate poetry quoted in text, to indicate alternative choices, and to separate figures in certain situations.

Use a slash, preceded and followed by a space, to mark the end of a line of poetry incorporated in text.

Shakespeare opens "The Passionate Pilgrim" with a seeming paradox: "When my love swears that she is made of truth, / I do believe her, though I know she lies."

Use a slash with no space before or after to separate alternatives.

an either/or situation

a pass/fail grading system

Use a slash to separate month, day, and year in a date given entirely in figures and to separate the numerator and the denominator in a typed fraction written entirely in figures. Use a hyphen to separate a whole number from its fraction.

7/16/04      2-1/16

# Standard Writing (Prose) Conventions

The conventions that govern spelling and the use of capital letters, hyphens, italics, numbers, and abbreviations help readers to understand your meaning.

## 40     Spelling

English spelling seems sometimes to defy reason. As the English language has borrowed and then absorbed words from other languages, it has assumed or adapted the spellings of the originals. Pronunciation is therefore often not a good key to spelling.

## 40a.  Basic spelling rules

**The *ie/ei* rule and its exceptions**  The familiar spelling rule "*i* before *e* except after *c* or when sounded like 'ay' as in *neighbor* and *weigh*" holds true in most cases.

> *i* before *e*: *belief, field, friend, mischief, piece, priest*
>
> *ei* after *c*: *ceiling, conceive, deceit, deceive, receipt*
>
> *ei* sounding like "ay": *eight, feign, freight, sleigh*

> ***Exceptions:***
>
> *ie* after *c*: *ancient, conscience, science, species*
>
> *ei* not after *c*: *caffeine, counterfeit, either, feisty, foreign, forfeit, height, leisure, neither, seize, weird*

### Suffixes

A suffix is a letter or a group of letters added to the end of a word that changes its meaning and sometimes its spelling.

**The suffixes *-cede, -ceed,* and *-sede***  The syllables *-cede, -ceed,* and *-sede* sound alike and are often confused.

> *-cede* (most common): *concede, intercede, precede*
>
> *-ceed: exceed, proceed, succeed*
>
> *-sede* (occurs in only one word): *supersede*

**Words ending in *y***  If the letter before the final *y* is a consonant, change the *y* to *i* before adding the suffix unless the suffix begins with *i*.

> friendly/friendlier     happy/happily
> apply/applying

***Exceptions:*** *dryly, shyly, wryly*

Keep the *y* if the letter before the *y* is a vowel.

convey/conveyed     annoy/annoyed

pay/payment

**Suffixes after words ending in e** When the suffix begins with a consonant, keep the final *e* before the suffix.

sure/surely     polite/politeness     hate/hateful

*Exceptions:* acknowledgment, argument, judgment, truly, wholly, awful, ninth

**Suffixes after words ending in a consonant** When adding a suffix to a word ending in a consonant, do not change the spelling, even if a double consonant results:

benefit/benefited     fuel/fueling     girl/girllike

**Final -ly or -ally** The suffixes –*ly* and –*ally* turn nouns into adjectives or adjectives into adverbs.

Add –*ly* to words that do not end in –*ic: absolutely, really.*

Add –*ally* to words that end in –*ic: basically, automatically.* (**Exception:** *publicly.*)

## Spelling rules for plurals

Most English nouns are made plural by adding –*s.* The following are exceptions to this rule.

**Nouns ending in ch, s, sh, or x** Add –*es* to form the plural of most nouns ending in *ch, s, sh,* or *x.*

church/churches     glass/glasses     box/boxes

**Nouns ending in y** Add –*s* to form the plural of nouns ending in *y* if the letter before the *y* is a vowel. Change the *y* to *i* and add –*es* if the letter before the *y* is a consonant.

day/days     alloy/alloys     melody/melodies

**Nouns ending in o** Add –*s* to form the plural of most nouns ending in *o.*

video/videos     trio/trios     inferno/infernos

For a few nouns that end in an *o* preceded by a consonant, form the plural by adding –*es.*

hero/heroes     potato/potatoes

For other nouns that end in *o*, the plural can be formed either way.

> zero/zeros/zeroes   tornado/tornados/tornadoes

**Compound nouns**   When a compound noun is written as one word, make only the last part of the compound plural.

> newspapers   notebooks

When a compound noun is written as separate words or hyphenated, make the word plural that expresses the main idea, usually a noun.

> attorneys general   brothers-in-law
> bath towels

# 41   Capitalization

A capital letter marks the beginning of a sentence and distinguishes names, titles, and certain other words.

## 41a.   The first word of a sentence

Use a capital letter at the beginning of a sentence or an intentional sentence fragment. (Capitalization is optional in a series of fragmentary questions, but be consistent.)

> What was the occasion? A holiday? A birthday?

## 41b.   Quotations

Capitalize the first word of a quoted sentence.

> "We'd like to talk to you," she said.

Do not capitalize the first word of the continuation of a quotation interrupted.

> "Unfortunately," he said, "we don't sell coffee."

### Lines of poetry

Poets make deliberate decisions about when and how they use capital letters. When quoting poetry, always follow the capitalization and punctuation of the original.

As e.e. cummings puts it, "one's not half two. It's two are halves of one:"

# 41c.  Proper nouns

Capitalize the names of particular persons, places, or things.

Toyota     the White House     the Gulf of Mexico

Do not capitalize the articles, conjunctions, or prepositions that appear within such names.

## Individual people and animals

Capitalize the names and nicknames of individual people and animals.

Michael Jordan     Buffalo Bill     Seabiscuit

Capitalize words describing family members only when they are used as names.

Mother/my mother     Aunt Carol/his aunt

## Religions and their members, deities, and sacred texts

Capitalize the names of religions, members of a religion, religious sects, deities, and sacred texts:

Judaism/Jews     Protestant     Allah     the Bible

## Nationalities, ethnic groups, and languages

Capitalize the names of nationalities, ethnic groups, and languages:

French     African American     Slavic

## Titles of people

Capitalize formal and courtesy titles and their abbreviations when they are used before a name and not set off by commas:

Gen. Wesley Clark     Professor Cox     Ms. Wu

Titles that indicate high office are often capitalized even when not directly followed by a name.

the Queen     the President of the United States

## Months, days of the week, and holidays

Capitalize the names of months, weekdays, and holidays.

August 12, 1914    Tuesday    Labor Day

Do not capitalize dates written out or the names of seasons.

the twentieth of April    spring

# Geographic names, place names, and directions

Capitalize the names of cities, states, countries, provinces, regions, bodies of water, and other geographic features.

Little Rock, Arkansas    the Western Hemisphere
Lake Erie    the Grand Canyon    the Midwest

Capitalize direction words when they indicate regions but not when they indicate compass directions.

the West    westerly

# Institutions, organizations, and businesses

Capitalize the names of institutions, organizations, and businesses.

Oberlin College    the Peace Corps
Federal Reserve Bank of New York

# Historical documents, events, and periods

Capitalize the names of historical documents and well-known events or periods.

the Constitution    the Stone Age
the Renaissance

# Movements in art, music, literature, and philosophy

Capitalize the names of artistic styles and schools of thought.

Impressionist painters    Romanticism

# Ships, aircraft, spacecraft, and trains

Capitalize the names of individual vehicles.

*Air Force One*    *Titanic*    *Voyager*

# Titles

Capitalize the first word, the last word, and all other words except articles, conjunctions, and prepositions in the titles and subtitles of books, plays, essays, stories, poems, movies, television programs, pieces of music, and works of art.

> *Pride and Prejudice*     *Beauty and the Beast*
> *La Traviata*     "The Wasteland"     *Friends*
> *Guernica*

Words joined by a hyphen are usually both capitalized, except for articles, conjunctions, and prepositions:

> Jack-in-the-Box restaurants     Forty-Second Street

## 41d.  Capitalization after colons

Capitalization is optional after a colon when the colon joins two independent clauses and the second clause contains the main point of the sentence.

> The senators' courage failed them: The health care bill was dead for another year.

Use capitals after a colon that introduces a numbered list of complete sentences (but not a list of phrases).

> His philosophy can be reduced to three basic rules:
> (1) Think for yourself. (2) Take care of your body.
> (3) Never hurt anyone.

## 42    Hyphens

Hyphens link words or parts of words to create new concepts and thus new meanings. They can also separate words into parts to clarify meaning. In addition, hyphens have many conventional uses in numbers, fractions, and units of measure.

## 42a.  Hyphens at the ends of lines

Use a hyphen to break a word that is too long to fit at the end of a line. The following guidelines will also help you determine how to hyphenate words:

**1.** Divide words only between pronounced syllables. Words of only one pronounced syllable—*eighth,* *through, dreamed, urged*—cannot be divided without suggesting an incorrect pronunciation.

**2.** Divide at prefixes or suffixes if possible. Try to leave both parts of a hyphenated word recognizable: not *an-tibody* but *anti-body,* not *ea-gerness* but *eager-ness.*

**3.** Don't leave just one letter at the end of a line or carry over only one or two letters to the next line.

**4.** A word with an internal double letter is usually divided between those letters: *syl-la-ble, wil-low;* but keep double letters together if they fall at the end of a base word, and divide the word before a suffix: *access-ible, assess-ment, will-ing.*

## 42b.  Hyphens after some prefixes

Use a hyphen when a prefix precedes a capitalized word or a date. The prefix itself is usually not capitalized.

> non-Catholic     pre-1994

Use a hyphen after a prefix attached to a term of two or more words.

> post-World War II     anti-labor union

Use a hyphen in almost all cases after the prefixes *all-, ex-, self-,* and *quasi-.*

> all-inclusive     ex-convict     self-hypnosis

To prevent misreading, hyphens are often used when a prefix ends with the same letter that begins the base word.

> anti-intellectual     co-ownership

When two prefixes apply to the same base word and are separated by a conjunction, use a hyphen and a space after the first prefix.

> We compared the pre- and postelection analyses.

## 42c.  Hyphens in compound words

Many compound words (closed compounds) are written as one word: *workhorse, schoolteacher.* Other compounds are written as two separate words (open compounds): *hope chest, lunch break, curtain rod.* And some compounds are hyphenated.

great-grandson     mother-in-law

stick-in-the-mud

Check the dictionary to see which compound words are written as one word and which are hyphenated. If you don't find a compound there, it is written as two words.

Hyphenate most compound nouns of three or more words.

jack-of-all-trades

Hyphenate to avoid misinterpretation.

small-business conferences

Do not hyphenate widely recognized open compounds.

post office box     high school student

Do not use a hyphen after an adverb ending in *ly*.

a highly paid worker

## 42d. Numbers, fractions, and units of measure

Hyphenate two-word numbers from twenty-one to ninety-nine. If you need to spell out higher numbers (see 44a), do not hyphenate before or after the words *hundred, thousand, million, billion,* and so on.

fifty-seven     twenty-two thousand

two hundred fifty-seven

six hundred twenty thousand

Hyphenate between the numerator and denominator of a spelled-out fraction unless one of them is already hyphenated.

one-half     two-thirds     twenty-one fiftieths

Hyphenate exact measurements used as modifiers; do not hyphenate measurements used as nouns.

My dump truck has a nine-cubic-yard bed.

My dump truck holds nine cubic yards.

Hyphenate ages used as modifiers or to designate persons; do not hyphenate an age used by itself.

my six-year-old son

my son, the six-year-old

My son is six years old.

# 43 Italics

To distinguish certain words in your text, use italics. In typed or handwritten papers, *underline* to indicate italics.

## 43a.  Italics for titles

Use italics for the titles of books, plays, operas and other long musical works, movies, recordings, newspapers, magazines, television and radio series, long poems considered to be independent works, and works of art.

> *Treasure Island* (book)
> "Powder and Arms" (chapter)
>
> *Leaves of Grass* (book of poems)
> "Song of Myself" (poem)
>
> *West Side Story* (musical)
> "Tonight" (song)
>
> *The Simpsons* (television series)
> "Homer Meets Godzilla" (episode)

Do not use italics (or quotation marks) for titles of sacred works, parts of sacred works, ancient manuscripts, or public documents.

> the Bible     the book of Genesis
> the Bill of Rights     the Civil Rights Act of 1964

## 43b.  Italics for the names of vehicles

Use italics for the official names of individual trains, ships, airplanes, and spacecraft.

> *City of New Orleans* (train)
> *Spirit of St. Louis* (airplane)

## 43c. Italics for foreign words

Many words in English have been absorbed by the language (lasagna) and do not require italics. Recently borrowed foreign words do (*pasticcio di faglioni*).

Use italics for the Latin names of plants and animals.

*Homo erectus* is an early human ancestor.

Use italics for words or numbers that stand only for themselves and for letters used as symbols in mathematics and other disciplines.

the term *liberal*          to substitute *y* for *u*

## 43d. Italics for emphasis

Use italics to indicate that a certain word or words should receive special attention or emphasis.

We all hear music in our heads, but how is music processed by the *brain*?

Be careful not to overuse italics. Too much emphasis of this sort can become monotonous.

**44** Numbers

When you use numbers to describe data and research findings that support your positions, follow the conventions of the discipline in which you are writing. For general purposes, the following guidelines will help you decide when to spell out numbers and when to use figures.

## 44a. Figures or spelled-out numbers?

Spell out numbers of one hundred or less and numbers that can be expressed in one or two words.

thirty students          three-fourths of the forest

517 students          52,331 trees

Use a combination of words and figures for round numbers over one million.

The US population exceeds 250 million.

Spell out any number that begins a sentence.

Five hundred twenty students attended the concert.

Treat consistently numbers that readers must compare.

Last year, 87 cats and 114 dogs were adopted.

In technical writing, use figures for numbers over nine and in all measurements:

12 clinical trials      3 pounds per square inch

## 44b.  Conventional uses of numbers

In all types of writing, convention requires the use of figures in certain situations.

### Dates

11 April 2001      the year 1616      July 16, 1927

### Addresses

2551 Polk Street, Apt. 3

San Francisco, CA 94109

### Abbreviations and symbols

3500 rpm      37°C      65 mph      $62.23
74%      53¢

If you spell out numbers, also spell out *percent, dollars,* and *cents.*

seventy-four percent      five dollars      fifty cents

### Time

12:15      2330 hours

Numbers used with *o'clock, past, to, till,* and *until* are generally written out as words: *seven o'clock, twenty past one.*

### Decimals and fractions

2.7 seconds      35.4 miles

### Cross-references and citations

Chapter 12      line 25      act 3, scene 2

## 44c. Singular and plural forms of numbers

When the word for a number is used as a plural noun without another number before it, use the plural form of the word. You may also need to use the word *of* after it.

> The report said there were only a few protesters at the nuclear power plant, but we saw hundreds of them.

When a word expressing a unit of weight, money, time, or distance is used with the word for a number, always use the singular form for both words.

> It was a three-hour movie.

# 45   Abbreviations

Abbreviations are used in tables, footnotes, endnotes, and bibliographies to speed up reading.

## 45a. Abbreviated titles and degrees

Abbreviate titles of address when they precede a full name, except for *President* and *Mayor,* which are never abbreviated.

> Mr. Samuel Taylor      Dr. Ellen Hunter

Abbreviate titles and degrees that follow a name, such as *Esq., MD, LLD, JD,* and *PhD* Use either a title (such as *Dr.*) or a degree (such as *MD*), but not both.

> Dr. Randall Marshall
>
> Randall Marshall, MD

Abbreviate generational titles such as *Jr.* and *Sr.* These were commonly set off by commas, but the modern trend is to use no punctuation except the period.

> He talked to Thomas Burke Jr. and to Karen Burke.

Do not abbreviate or capitalize titles that are not used with a proper name: *assistant professor of chemistry.*

Except for *Mr., Ms., Mrs.,* and *Dr.,* do not abbreviate titles that appear before a surname alone.

Professor Greenberg     Senator McCain

## 45b. Abbreviations with numbers

### Time

Use a.m. and p.m. for specific times of day.

3:45 p.m.     12 noon

### Year

Use BC (*before Christ*) and AD (*anno Domini*) for calendar years. Only AD precedes the year. To avoid religious reference, you may use BCE (*before the Common Era*) and CE (*Common Era*).

## 45c. Degrees, numbers, and units of measure

When writing out temperatures, use °F for *degrees Fahrenheit* and °C for *degrees Celsius.* Use *no.* or *No.* for *number.* Use *mph* for *miles per hour.*

Today's high will be around 92°F.

Fill out this form using a No. 2 pencil.

The speed limit on most city streets is 30 mph.

In scientific and technical writing, abbreviate units of measure, usually without periods, especially if they are metric measurements.

He added 200 mg of sodium cyanate.

## 45d. Symbols

Use symbols for degrees (°), percents (%), and dollars ($) when they are used with figures. Spell out symbols in words when the numbers are spelled as words. Be consistent.

It was 30°C and sunny 75% of the time.

## 45e. Abbreviated geographic names

Abbreviate geographic names when addressing mail. Use the US Postal Service state abbreviations with ZIP codes.

100 W. Glengarry Ave.
Birmingham, MI 48009

When presenting a full address in text, do not abbreviate anything except the state name before the ZIP code. Do not abbreviate place names when you give a general location.

He lives at 11 West Sixth Street, Harrisburg, PA 17102.

She was born in Madison, Wisconsin.

## 45f.  Common Latin abbreviations

Use common Latin abbreviations in documentation and notes, but write out their English equivalents in your text.

| ABBREVIATION | LATIN TERM | MEANING |
|---|---|---|
| *c.* or *ca.* | *circa* | about |
| *cf.* | *confer* | compare |
| *e.g.* | *exempli gratia* | for example |
| *et al.* | *et alii* | and others |
| *etc.* | *et cetera* | and so forth |
| *i.e.* | *id est* | that is |
| *NB* | *nota bene* | note well |

## 45g.  Acronyms and initials

Make sure that any acronyms and initial abbreviations you use are familiar to your readers. If you have any doubts, give the full name the first time, followed by the abbreviation or acronym in parentheses.

Starting in 1947, commerce was governed by a set of treaties called the General Agreement on Tariffs and Trade (GATT).

For rules on formatting acronyms and initial abbreviations, see 33a.

## 46  Document Preparation

Well-prepared documents are well received.

# 46a. Preparing final copy

College instructors commonly request that academic papers follow specific style guidelines such as MLA, APA, or CM, which are covered in Chapters 53 through 66. However, if your instructor does not specify a style or if you are writing for business or publishing purposes, the following guidelines will be helpful:

- Print on clean $8\frac{1}{2}$-by-11-inch white paper in a readable font with 1-inch margins all around.
- Double-space papers unless instructed otherwise.
- Include name, instructor name, course title, and date on the first page, flush with the upper left-hand margin. Double-space.
- Center the title on the next line, using initial capital letters for all main words. Double-space.
- Indent the first word of each paragraph five spaces.
- Space once after each word and each sentence.
- Set off quotations of four lines or more in double-spaced block format, indented ten spaces.
- Number each page in the upper right-hand corner, $\frac{1}{2}$ inch from the top unless otherwise instructed. Include your last name one space before each page number.

# 46b. Proofreading

Proofreading is the process of finding and correcting errors in typing, spelling, punctuation, and mechanics. Plan to proofread twice: once on the edited draft from which you will prepare your final copy and once on the final copy itself.

- Read your paper aloud to give you a chance to hear anything that isn't clear and natural.
- Ask someone else to proofread your final draft.
- Read your own paper backward, starting with the last word and work back, one word at a time, to the first, using a ruler to focus on a single line.
- Use your computer's spell checker, but note that spell checkers do not catch wrong or omitted words.
- Use standard proofreading symbols to mark your paper for correction later.

# Research Writing

A research project begins with a question that (1) interests you, (2) doesn't have an easy answer, and (3) can be examined in the time and with the resources available. If you have a tentative answer to your question, formulate a working thesis to help guide your research (see Chapter 12). If research leads to more questions or suggests a more interesting topic, redirect your investigation and revise your working thesis.

# 47 Library Research

The college library is the heart of the academic community and the most reliable source of credible information in all academic subjects. Many informative resources are also available on the Internet and in the field, but their reliability varies immensely (see Chapters 48 and 49). In contrast, resources selected by professional librarians are screened for authenticity and credibility. Librarians can save you precious time by showing you the most helpful resources. If you are not sure how to begin, follow this research plan.

1. Visit the **reference room** to discuss a research plan with a reference librarian. Here you can also locate background information, definitions, and basic facts in appropriate dictionaries, encyclopedias, guides, and bibliographies. General reference works help begin, but not complete, serious academic investigations.

2. Search **periodicals** (magazines and journals) first, to locate more up-to-date information than books can supply. To find journal articles on your topic, begin with an online index such as *Expanded Academic ASAP,* which provides access to citations in both scholarly journals and general-interest magazines on a variety of topics. This database, available only electronically, covers 5,200 scholarly and general-interest periodicals from 1980 to the present in a wide variety of subject areas. About half of the content is full-text. Also look in *Academic Search Premier,* a database containing full-text articles from 3900 scholarly journals dating as far back as 1975. If you cannot locate useful databases, tell your reference librarian what you are looking for and inquire about the best method to access the most recent periodical information.

3. Move to your library's **catalog** to locate library books by author, title, subject, or key word. Most online catalogs allow searching with partial

information; if you know only the first two words of a title, the computer will generate a list of all works beginning with those words. The computer search can identify other related work, other titles by the same author, where to locate the book, and whether or not it is checked out. It is often worthwhile, also, to peruse library shelves containing books with the same call numbers in order to find related works.

4. Develop a **working bibliography.** Make an alphabetical list of all the works consulted (or you plan to consult) on 3-by-5 index cards or in a computer file (especially if you use a database manager)—both allow for easy alphabetizing, which is useful to create a reference page for your paper. For each source, record the following information:

**BOOKS**

| | |
|---|---|
| 1. Call number or other location information | 4. Editor or translator |
| 2. Full name(s) of author(s) | 5. Place of publication |
| 3. Full title and subtitle | 6. Publisher |
| | 7. Date of publication |

**PERIODICALS**

| | |
|---|---|
| 1. Full name(s) of author(s) | 5. Periodical date |
| 2. Full title and subtitle of article | 6. Page numbers |
| 3. Periodical title | 7. Location |
| 4. Periodical volume and number | |

5. Take **notes** on cards or files separate from bibliography cards, putting one bit of information or one idea on a card—a strategy that will help you locate, shuffle, and rearrange ideas as you shape your paper. Each note should contain the following information:

| | |
|---|---|
| 1. Author and precise title of the source | 4. Information quoted, paraphrased, or summarized |
| 2. Page numbers | 5. Notes (in brackets or parentheses) on how you might use or cross-reference to other material |
| 3. Brief statement of the source topic | |

# 48    Internet Research

Using the Internet for academic research requires good search skills and the ability to evaluate sources for their relevance and reliability. This chapter focuses on how to search for information; Chapter 50 focuses on evaluating Internet sources.

## 48a.  Select a search engine

Different search engines compile different databases, so the same search with a different engine may bring different results. Search engines come in two types. *Crawlers* are automated programs that evaluate sites, reading every page of a site, counting, for example, the number of times key terms appear and noting the number of other sites that point to it. The following are reliable crawlers:

> Google *<http://www.google.com>*
>
> HotBot *<http://www.hotbot.com>*
>
> Teoma *<http://www.teoma.com>*

The other main type of search routine is a *directory,* an index organized by subject in the manner of a library subject catalog or the telephone Yellow Pages. Directories are usually compiled by human editors or refined by humans from a computer-generated database. Popular directories include these:

> Yahoo *<http://www.yahoo.com>*
>
> About *<http://about.com>*
>
> Google *<http://www.google.com>*
> (click the Directory tab)

A *metasearch engine* such as Dogpile at *<http://www.dogpile.com>* feeds your search terms to several search engines at once.

For more lists of search sites and tips on searching, search on *search engines,* or visit SearchEngineWatch at *<http://searchenginewatch.com>* or SearchEngines.com at *<http://www.searchengines.com>*.

# 48b.  Limit your search

When you enter a word or phrase in a search engine, the program retrieves a list of pages that contain your search terms. Sometimes that list is impossibly long. Searching for *music* on Google locates 108 million pages; limiting the search to *classical music* yields a mere 4.5 million. Even searching for *composer Edvard Grieg* retrieves 6,560 pages. Narrowing further to *composer Grieg biography* yields manageable and useful results.

Every search engine has an "advanced search" or help page that tells how it works and what special tools are available. For example, if you enter more than one word in Google, by default it returns only pages that contain *all* your search terms. That's why *classical music* yields fewer pages than *music* or *classical.* To search within those results, simply add another term: *American classical music.*

Some search engines use *stemming,* a way of searching for related words at the same time. Searching for *parent* would also produce references to *parents* and *parental.* Others let you use an asterisk to include multiple forms: *parent*\*. On engines that do not use stemming, you must search separately: *parents' rights, parent's rights,* and *parental rights.* Consult the help page of each search engine for details.

Search engines allow you to combine terms in logical ways. Using what is called Boolean logic, you can search for *rights and parent's or parents' or parental* and accomplish the same thing as three separate searches. You can also exclude terms: *rights and parent's or parents' or parental not grandparents' or grandparent's.*

Most search engines ignore prepositions (*in, on, around*) and other small, common words. To guarantee that a word is included, put a space and plus sign in front of it: *breakfast +in bed* yields more specific results than *breakfast in bed* but doesn't eliminate all the *bed and breakfast* results. To search for an exact phrase, put it in quotation marks: "*breakfast in bed.*"

# 48c.  Search Web sites

When you find a Web site devoted to your topic, look for links to other sites. Chances are the author of the site has listed sources of related information. If you find a dead link, check your typing and try again. Then shorten the Web address to its most basic components. And be sure to examine several different sites on the same subject that may provide different information or have different degrees of reliability.

In addition to focused searching, leave some time for open-ended "surfing" that may turn up still more useful sites. Here are some specialized, academic, and library resources.

- Amazon.com, *<http://www.amazon.com>*: Lists books in print and out-of-print titles, including publication data and reviews, and suggests related titles to use for purchasing books or finding them in a library.

- Bartleby.com, *<http://www.bartleby.com>*: Offers complete, searchable text of works of literature, poetry, and criticism.

- Biographical Dictionary, *<http://www.s9.com/biography>*

- CIA World Factbook, *<http://www.cia.gov/cia/publications/factbook>*: Provides comprehensive information on every country.

- Infoplease, *<http://www.infoplease.com>*: Online almanac with topics from architecture to biography to historical statistics to weather.

- The Internet Public Library, *<http://www.ipl.org>*

- Learn the Net Inc., *<http://www.learnthenet.com/english/index.html>*: Offers Web tours and training.

- RefDesk.com, *<http://www.refdesk.com>*: Noncommercial site dedicated to research of all kinds.

- Reference.com, *<http://www.reference.com>*: Has dictionaries, thesauruses, encyclopedias, and more.

## 48d.  Search with e-mail

Once you have an e-mail address, you can correspond with millions of other people who have useful research information. To locate an e-mail address, try Search.com at *<http://www.search.com/search?channel=10>* or an address metasearch at *<http://www.addresses.com>*. People often post their e-mail addresses on their own Web sites, and institutions such as universities often have faculty e-mail directories on their Web pages. If you know someone who works at an institution but can't find his or

her e-mail address, try writing to the contact address provided on the Web site.

## 48e. Document your search

In a research notebook, record search terms you use, sites
you visit, and e-mail contacts. Print copies of useful pages
or information, and if your printer doesn't automatically
print Web URLs, record them as well as date and time in
your notebook. If you're using your own computer, save
useful locations in your browser's Bookmark or Favorites
file.

## 49     Field Research

Depending on your research question, you may need to
conduct research outside the library and away from computers. Field research simply means visiting places (a
lakeshore, a downtown) or people (a biologist, a worker)
and taking careful notes. Field research gets you fresh, local
information about people, places, events, or objects to
provide you with original data to incorporate into research
papers.

## 49a. Site observation tips

The following suggestions will increase your chances of
successful site visits.

- **Select relevant sites.** When doing research at local
  sites, visit places that will be the primary focus of your
  paper or offer supplementary details to support your
  major points.

- **Do homework.** Consult reference room or online
  sources such as encyclopedias, dictionaries, and
  atlases to orient you toward and inform yourself about
  the places you will visit.

- **Call ahead.** Find out directions and convenient times
  to visit and let site people know you are coming.

- **Bring a notebook with a stiff cover.** It will help
  you write while walking or standing. Double-entry

notebooks allow you to record facts in one column and your reactions in the other.

- **Use a handheld tape recorder** for on-site dictation to supplement or replace written notes.

- **Review, transcribe, and rewrite** both written and dictated notes within twenty-four hours after your visit.

- **Sketch, photograph, or videotape** useful visual information.

## 49b.  Interview tips

The following suggestions will increase your chances for successful personal interviews.

- **Select relevant people.** Determine what information you need, who is likely to have it, and how to approach them.

- **Call ahead for an appointment.** Let your subject know when you are coming or when appointments need changing.

- **Do homework.** Consult library or Internet sources for background information on your interview subject.

- **Prepare questions in advance.** Ask general questions to establish context; ask specific questions to become more informed.

- **Ask open questions** to elicit general information: *How did that situation develop? What are your plans for the future?*

- **Ask closed questions** when you need facts or concrete details to support a point: *When did that policy begin? What is the name of the district manager?*

- **Ask follow-up questions** if answers are incomplete or confusing. Get all the information possible at one sitting.

- **Use silence.** If your subject does not respond right away, allow time for him or her to think, recall, or reflect before filling the silence with another question.

- **Read body language.** Notice how your subject acts: Does the person look you in the eyes? Fidget? Look bored? Smile?—actions that suggest whether someone is speaking honestly, avoiding your question, or tiring fast. Including descriptions of body language along with conversation adds interest to your paper.

- **Use a tape recorder.** Ask permission in advance, and make sure your equipment works. Continue to make written notes of conversation highlights to help you remember questions that occur while your subject is talking and to describe the subject's appearance and manner.

- **Confirm important assertions.** Read back important or controversial statements to check for accuracy and allow for further explanation.

# 50 Evaluating Research Sources

Good sources inform your papers and make them believable. To determine that a source is good, you must answer yes to two questions: (1) Is the source credible? (2) Is it useful in my paper? This chapter provides guidelines for evaluating the credibility and usefulness of sources found in the library, on the Internet, and in the field.

## 50a. Evaluating library sources

The sources you find in a college library are generally credible because experts have already screened them. The books, periodicals, documents, special collections, and electronic sources have been recommended for library acquisition by scholars, researchers, and librarians with special expertise in the subject areas the library catalogs. However, just because *some* authorities judged a source to be credible *at one time* does not necessarily mean it still is or that it's the best available or that it's not contested or that it's especially useful for the paper you are writing. Two of the main reasons for distrusting a source found in the library have to do with *time* (when was it judged true?) and *perspective* (who said it was true, and for what reason?).

## Identifying dated sources

Most library documents include their date of publication inside the cover of the document itself, and in most cases this will be a fact you can rely on. In some cases, such as articles first published in one place and reprinted in an anthology, you may have to dig for the original date, but it's usually there (check the permissions page).

One of the main reasons any source may become un-reliable—and less than credible—is the passage of time. For example, any geographic, political, or statistical information true for 1950 or even 2004 will be more or less changed by the time you examine it—in many cases, radically so. (Just look at atlas or encyclopedia entries for Africa or Asia from 1950!) Yet at one time this source was judged to be accurate.

Check the critical reception of books when published by reading reviews in *Book Review Digest* (also available online); often you can tell whether the critical argument over the book twenty years ago is still relevant or has been bypassed by other events and publications.

At the same time, dated information has all sorts of uses. In spite of being "dated," works such as the Bible, the *I Ching,* the novels of Virginia Woolf, and the beliefs of Malcolm X are valuable for many reasons. In studying change over time, old statistical information is crucial. Knowing the source date lets you decide whether to use it.

## Identifying perspective

Who created the source, and with what intention? Why did the person or organization write, construct, compile, record, or otherwise create this source in the first place? This second question is difficult to answer by reviewing the source itself. Although most library texts include the dates they were published, few accurately advertise their purpose or the author's point of view—and when they do, this information cannot always be believed.

To evaluate the usefulness of a text, ask questions about (1) the assumptions it makes, (2) the evidence it presents, and (3) the reasoning that holds it together. Finding answers to these critical questions reveals an author's bias.

■ What is this writer's purpose—scholarly analysis, political advocacy, entertainment, or something else?

- Can you classify the author's point of view (liberal, conservative, radical) and differentiate it from other points of view?

- What does the writer assume about the subject or about the audience? (What does unexplained jargon tell you?)

- How persuasive is the evidence? Which statements are facts, which inferences drawn from facts, and which matters of opinion? (See Chapter 13.)

- Are there relevant points you are aware of that the writer *doesn't* mention? What does this tell you?

- How compelling is the logic? Are there places where it doesn't make sense? How often?

Your answers to these questions should reveal the degree to which you accept the author's conclusions.

## Cross-referencing sources

Although at first it may seem daunting to answer all these questions, have patience and give the research process the time it needs. On a relatively new subject, the more you learn, the more you learn! The more differences you note, the more answers to the questions you find, and the more you know if a source might be useful.

## 50b. Evaluating electronic sources

You need to apply the same critical scrutiny to Internet sources as to library sources, only more so. With no editor, librarian, or review board to screen for accuracy, reliability, or integrity, anyone with a computer and a modem can publish personal opinions, commercial pitches, bogus claims, bomb-making instructions, or smut on the Web. Although the Internet is a marvelous source of research information, it's also a trap for unwary researchers. So in addition to timeliness and perspective, what do you need to look out for? First, look at the electronic address (URL) to identify the type of organization sponsoring the site.

- ~      personal home page
- .aero      aviation group
- .biz      business
- .com      commerce or business

- .coop     credit union or rural co-op
- .edu     educational institution
- .gov     government institution
- .info     information source open to the public
- .mil     military institution
- .museum     accredited museum
- .name     second-level name
- .net     news or other network
- .org     nonprofit agency
- .pro     professional organization

Each abbreviation suggests the potential bias in sites: **.com** and **.biz** sites are usually selling something; **.coop** and **.pro** may be selling something but may have a stronger interest in promoting the public welfare; **.mil** and **.org** are nonprofit, but each has an agenda to promote and defend; **.edu, .gov, .museum,** and **.net** should be neutral and unbiased, but they still need careful checking; and **.info, .name,** or ~ could be anyone with any idea.

Second, ask as many critical questions as you would of a library source. An easy way to do this is to ask the *reporter's questions* (*who, what, where, when, why,* and *how*—see Chapter 10) and see what the answers tell you.

### WHO IS THE SITE AUTHOR?

- Look for a person's name. Check the top or the bottom of the page.
- Look for credentials: scholar, scientist, doctor, college degrees, experience?
- If there is no personal name, look for a sponsoring organization. What does it stand for?
- Look for links to the author or agency's home page.
- Look for a way to contact the author or agency by e-mail, phone, or mail to ask further questions.
- If you cannot tell who created the site or contact its sponsors, site credibility is low. Don't rely on this site's information.

### WHAT IDEAS OR INFORMATION DOES THE SITE PRESENT?

- Look for concepts and terminology you know.
- Look for facts versus inferences, opinions, and speculation. Be especially wary of opinion and speculation.

- Look for balanced versus biased points of view. What tips you off? Which would you trust more?

- Look for missing information. Why is it not there?

- Look for advertising. Is it openly identified and separated from factual material?

### HOW IS THE INFORMATION PRESENTED?

- Look at the care with which the site is constructed, an indication of the education level of the author. If it contains spelling and grammar errors or is loaded with unexplained jargon, do you trust it? Will your readers?

- Look at the clarity of the graphics and/or sound features. Do they contribute to the content of the site?

- Look for links to other sites that suggest a connected, comprehensive knowledge base.

### WHERE DOES THE INFORMATION COME FROM?

- Identify the source of the site: *.edu, .gov, .com,* and so on (see earlier).

- Identify the source of site facts. Do you trust it?

- Look for prior appearance as a print source. Are you familiar with it? Is it reputable?

### WHEN WAS THE SITE CREATED?

- Look for creation date or the date of latest update; a date more than a year old suggests a site is not current.

- Look for absence of a creation date. Would lack of a date affect the reliability of the information?

- Look at whether or not the site is complete or still under construction. If incomplete, note that.

### WHY IS THE INFORMATION PRESENTED?

- Look for clues to the agenda of the site. Is it to inform? Persuade? Entertain? Sell? Are you buying?

- Does getting information from the site cost money? (You should not have to pay for reference material for a college paper.)

## Identifying anonymous Internet sources

You can find out who owns a domain name—and often get contact addresses for owners or officers of a site—at the InterNIC WHOIS site run by Network Solutions Inc., the company responsible for administering most domain names: *<http://www.internic.net>*. But a site that makes you search for such information, rather than providing it for you, should not inspire confidence.

## 50c.  Evaluating field sources

Unfortunately, the reliability and credibility of field sources is problematic because it is often more difficult for readers to track down field sources than textual sources. An interview is a onetime event, so a subject available one day may not be the next. A location providing information one day may change or become off limits the next. To examine field sources critically, you need to freeze them and make them hold still. Here's what to do.

### Interviews

With the subject's permission, use a tape recorder and transcribe the whole session. Once an interview is taped, apply to it the critical questions you would a written source (see earlier). If you cannot tape-record, take careful notes, review main points with your subject before the interview ends, and apply these same critical questions.

### Site observations

To freeze a site, make photographic or video records of what it looked like and what you found, in addition to taking copious notes about time, including details of location, size, shape, color, number, and so forth. If you cannot make photo records, sketch, draw, or diagram what you find. Pictures and careful verbal descriptions add credibility to papers by providing specific details that would be difficult to invent had the writer not been present. Even if you don't use them directly in your paper, visual notes will jog your memory of other important site events.

### Personal bias

Evaluating in-person observations is complicated because you are both the creator and the evaluator of the material. First, you shape interview material by the questions you ask, the manner in which you conduct the interview, and the language of your notes. Second, you shape on-site material by where you look, what you notice, and the language of your notes. In other words, in field research, the manner in which you collect and record information is most likely to introduce the most difficult bias to control, your own.

# 51 Using Research Sources

As you prepare to compose, assess all the information you've found and decide which sources to use and how. In other words, you need to synthesize unorganized raw material into an original, coherent paper.

To synthesize notes in preparation for writing, (1) look for connections among similar statements made by several sources, (2) look for contradictions between and among sources, and (3) marshal the evidence that furthers your paper's goal and set aside evidence that doesn't—everything you've collected cannot possibly fit and shouldn't.

Beware of constructing a source-driven paper, one whose direction is dictated by what you've found rather than what you are curious about and want to explore and examine. If you need more evidence, go get it rather than settling for answers to a question you haven't asked or faking it. Source-driven papers are obvious and odious to practiced instructors in every discipline.

Most research notes exist in three basic formats: *direct quotation, paraphrase,* and *summary.* Field notes may be more rambling. Whenever you quote, paraphrase, or summarize, be sure to document the source to the best of your ability.

## 51a. Quotations

**Direct quotations** reproduce an author's or speaker's exact words. Direct quotations help you examine other people's ideas or add credibility to your own ideas. However, using too many quotations reduces your own authorial input, suggesting too much reliance on others' thoughts. Too many quotations can also be distracting; if you have more than two or three per page, it suggests that you haven't introduced, explained, or interpreted them well. In addition, long quotations slow readers down and invite skimming. Use only as much of a quotation as you need to support your point.

Using *brief* quotations gains space and readability. You can't change what a source says, but you can control how much of it you use. When you shorten a quotation, be careful not to change or distort its meaning. If you omit words within a quotation, indicate the missing words with ellipsis points (. . .) (see 39c). Any changes or additions must be indicated by including the new words in brackets.

**ORIGINAL**
*The human communication environment has acquired biological complexity and planetary scale, but there are no scientists or activists monitoring it, theorizing about its health, or mounting campaigns to protect its resilience.*

Stewart Brand, *The Media Lab* 258

**INACCURATE QUOTATION (CHANGED MEANING)**
In <u>The Media Lab</u>, Stewart Brand describes "biological complexity" as a hazard to scientists.

**ACCURATE QUOTATION**
In <u>The Media Lab</u>, Stewart Brand notes the growth and complexity of the modern telecommunications environment. But nobody is "monitoring it . . . to protect its resilience" (258).

## Integrating quotations into your paper

Integrate direct quotations smoothly into your paper by providing an explanatory tag *at the beginning* to explain the quote and show its relevance. Brief quotations (four or fewer typed lines) should be embedded in the main body of your paper and enclosed in quotation marks. The short quotation in the following passage is from a personal interview:

> Photo editor Tom Brennan took ten minutes to sort through my images and then told me, "Most photography editors wouldn't take more than two minutes to look at a portfolio."

Set off quotations of five lines or longer in block format, indented ten spaces (see Chapter 54, item 12).

## Introducing quotations

Introduce who is speaking, what the quotation refers to, and where it is from. If the author is well known, be sure to mention his or her name as part of the signal phrase.

In <u>Walden</u>, Henry David Thoreau claims, "The mass of men lead lives of quiet desperation" (5).

If the title of your written work is well known, you can introduce a quotation with the title rather than the author's name, as long as the reference is clear.

<u>Walden</u> sets forth one individual's antidote against the "lives of quiet desperation" led by the working class in mid-nineteenth-century America (Thoreau 5).

## Signal phrases

A signal phrase should accurately reflect the intention of the source. Unless the context requires a past-tense verb, use the present. To vary the verb in your signal phrase, consider the synonyms such as *admits, argues, believes, claims, comments, finds, illustrates, observes, reports, reveals, says, speculates, suggests, wonders,* and *writes.*

## Explaining quotations

Sometimes a quotation needs to be explained to ensure clarity, as in this final sentence:

In <u>A Sand County Almanac</u>, Aldo Leopold invites urban readers to confront what they lose by living in the city: "There are two spiritual dangers in not owning a farm. One is the danger of supposing that breakfast comes from the grocery, and the other that heat comes from the furnace" (6). **In other words, Leopold sees city dwellers as dangerously ignorant of how their basic needs are met.**

You may also need to clarify what a word or reference means. Do this by using square brackets. In the following passage, it's unclear *who* will shrink.

**UNCLEAR**
Observing the remains of earwigs, sow bugs, moths, and spiders, Dillard reminds us that everything is changing, even in death: "Next week, if the other bodies are any indication, he will be shrunken and gray, webbed to the floor with dust" (279).

**CLEAR**
Observing the remains of earwigs, sow bugs, moths, and spiders, Dillard reminds us that

everything is changing, even in death: "Next week, if the other bodies are any indication, [the earwig] will be shrunken and gray, webbed to the floor with dust" (279).

## Adjusting grammar in quoted passages

A passage containing a quotation must follow all the rules of grammatical sentence structure—tenses should be consistent, verbs and subjects should agree, and so on. If the form of the passage doesn't fit the grammar of your own sentences, change your sentences, or slightly alter the quotation. Use this last option sparingly, and always indicate any changes with brackets.

### GRAMMATICALLY INCOMPATIBLE

If Thoreau thought that in his day, "The mass of men lead lives of quiet desperation" (<u>Walden</u> 5), what would he say of the masses today?

### GRAMMATICALLY COMPATIBLE

If Thoreau thought that in his day the masses led "lives of quiet desperation" (<u>Walden</u> 5), what would he say of the masses today?

### GRAMMATICALLY COMPATIBLE

In the nineteenth century, Thoreau stated, "The mass of men lead lives of quiet desperation" (<u>Walden</u> 5). What would he say of the masses today?

### GRAMMATICALLY COMPATIBLE

If Thoreau thought that in his day the "mass of men [led] lives of quiet desperation" (<u>Walden</u> 5), what would he say of the masses today?

- Quote directly when you cannot express the ideas better yourself.
- Quote directly when the original words are especially clear, powerful, or vivid.
- Quote directly when you want an authority's exact words to back you up.

## 51b.  Paraphrasing

When you **paraphrase,** you restate an author's words in your own words to make the ideas clearer or to adapt them to your purpose. Paraphrases should generally re-create the original source's order, structure, and emphasis and include most details. A paraphrase should be clearer, but not necessarily briefer, than the original.

A paraphrase should neither distort meaning nor too closely follow the sentence patterns of the original (see Chapter 52). Follow these rules when you paraphrase:

- Check definitions of all words you don't know.
- Recast ideas in your own words.
- Don't paraphrase one sentence at a time—go for the meaning of the whole passage.
- Include any context necessary to explain the passage.

> **ORIGINAL**
> *The human communication environment has acquired biological complexity and planetary scale, but there are no scientists or activists monitoring it, theorizing about its health, or mounting campaigns to protect its resilience.*
> Stewart Brand, *The Media Lab* 258

> **ACCURATE PARAPHRASE**
> Brand points out that our "communication environment" is as complex and vast as any ecosystem on the planet, yet no one monitors this environment to keep track of its growth and warn us if something is about to go wrong (258).

## 51c. Summarizing

To **summarize** is to condense the main ideas of a passage into your own words. A summary includes only the essentials of the original, not the specific details. The length of the original source has no bearing on the length of your summary. You may summarize a paragraph, a chapter, or even a book in a few sentences. The more material summarized, however, the more general and abstract it becomes, so be careful not to distort the meaning of the original.

> **ORIGINAL**
> *The human communication environment has acquired biological complexity and planetary scale, but there are no scientists or activists monitoring it, theorizing about its health, or mounting campaigns to protect its resilience.*
> Stewart Brand, *The Media Lab* 258

**INACCURATE SUMMARY**

The current telecommunications networks compose a nasty, unchangeable, and inescapable environment (Brand 258).

**ACCURATE SUMMARY**

Telecommunications networks have expanded so rapidly that monitoring and controlling them are difficult (Brand 258).

- Summarize to convey the main points of an original source but not the supporting details.
- Summarize to provide an overview or an interesting aside without digressing from your paper's focus.
- Summarize to condense lengthy notes into tight sentences.

# 52　Avoiding Plagiarism

The rule is simple: When, in writing a paper, you use other people's ideas or language, you must give credit to the authors whose ideas and words you have used. If you don't, you have stolen their ideas or words and are guilty of **plagiarism.** In Western culture, plagiarism is a serious offense, one that has cost writers, reporters, artists, musicians, and scientists their reputations, jobs, and vast sums of money. Plagiarism is especially serious within academic communities, where the generation of original research, ideas, and words is the central mission of the institution.

The Internet has made the copying of research sources especially easy, which saves researchers an enormous amount of time. However, Internet copying has also made plagiarism easy. To avoid plagiarizing, you need to know exactly what plagiarism is and how to avoid committing it.

## 52a.　What plagiarism *is*

Plagiarism is putting one's name on a paper written by a friend and turning it in. It's buying a term paper from a term-paper factory and pretending that you have written it. It's downloading a report from the Internet and substituting your name for the original author's name. In any of these flagrant examples, the intent to plagiarize is deliberate and obvious, something that serious and honorable students would never do.

However, plagiarism also occurs when well-meaning students get lazy, careless, or pressured in their note-taking, composing, or documenting. Here are three examples of *unintentional* plagiarism: (1) A student copies a passage word-for-word from an Internet site and pastes it word-for-word into a paper, but without quotation marks or author attribution. (2) A student summarizes, but does not directly quote, a published author's idea and omits both the author's name and the book's title. (3) A student credits an author's idea in a signal phrase ("According to . . .") but omits quotation marks around the author's exact phrases. None of these may be intentional, but each is an act of plagiarism, and each could be avoided by clearer knowledge and more careful research practice.

## 52b.  What plagiarism *is not*

Writers don't need to attribute everything they write or say to specific sources. For example, what we call *common knowledge* does not need documentation. You do not need to credit common historical, cultural, or geographic information that an educated American adult can be expected to know. Nor do you need to attribute to specific authorities the factual information that appears in multiple sources, such as the dates of historical events (the sack of Rome in AD 410, the adoption of the Declaration of Independence on July 4, 1776), the names and locations of states and cities, the general laws of science (gravity, motion), or statements of well-known theories (feminism, supply and demand, evolution).

You don't need to document current knowledge in widespread use in your own culture (global warming, cloning, urban sprawl). Nor do you need to document what is well known in the field in which you are writing or most basic information that can be found in textbooks and lectures. For example, you need not document the term *libido* or *superego* (associated with Sigmund Freud) in a psychology paper or *myth* or *postmodern* in an English, history, art, or philosophy paper. In other words, within a given interpretive community, basic ideas and knowledge can be assumed to be the common property of all members of that community. However, specific positions or interpretations within a community do need to be specifically identified.

# 52c.  Recognizing and avoiding plagiarism

If the author of an article, book, or Web site offers unique opinions or interpretations about any type of common knowledge (see the examples in Chapter 51), these should be credited using the proper documentation style. For example, if you were writing a paper in a film course about comic book heroes portrayed in the movies, you might want to use this passage in Roger Ebert's review of *Spider-Man* for the *Chicago Sun Times* on May 3, 2002:

> *Remember the first time you saw the characters defy gravity in* Crouching Tiger, Hidden Dragon? *They transcended gravity, but they didn't dismiss it: They seemed to possess weight, dimension and presence. Spider-Man as he leaps across the rooftops is landing too lightly, rebounding too much like a bouncing ball. He looks like a video game figure, not like a person having an amazing experience.*

Ebert's review is readily available on the Internet, accessed via the Internet Movie Database at **<http://www.imdb.com>**, so it's easy to copy parts of it and paste them directly into a research paper. Source information must accompany all such "borrowed" material, in the format prescribed by the discipline in which you are writing (see Chapters 53–66). If you do not follow proper citation guidelines, you might inadvertently plagiarize, as the following examples illustrate.

- It is plagiarism if you cut and paste the *Spider-Man* passage into your paper without acknowledging that it was written by Roger Ebert.

  To fix, identify the author in a signal phrase ("According to Roger Ebert . . ."), put the passage in quotation marks, and tell where the passage came from.

- It is plagiarism if you write:

  > The problem with Spider-Man is the video game quality of the characters who bound from roof to roof and don't seem to be affected by gravity—unlike the more realistic figures in the movie Crouching Tiger, Hidden Dragon.

In this case, you have used Ebert's idea in clearly identifiable ways without quoting Ebert directly, but also without crediting him.

To fix, identify the author in a signal phrase ("According to Roger Ebert . . .") and tell where the passage came from.

■ It is plagiarism if you use key portions of Ebert's exact language from the passage without using quotation marks:

> Roger Ebert claims that the characters in Crouching Tiger, Hidden Dragon transcended gravity, but they didn't dismiss it.

Although Ebert is credited with the idea, he is not credited with the language.

To fix, put quotation marks around the borrowed words:

> Roger Ebert claims that the characters in Crouching Tiger, Hidden Dragon "transcended gravity, but they didn't dismiss it."

---

### Guidelines for Avoiding Plagiarism

■ For all copied sources, note *who said what, where,* and *when.*

■ When using quoted material, do not distort the author's meaning.

■ Print out and save at least the first page of all online material.

■ Copy identifying information on all copied or printed source pages.

■ Place all borrowed language in quotation marks.

■ Identify all borrowed ideas with appropriate references.

■ In writing a paraphrase or summary, use your own words.

# MLA Documentation

The most common and most economical form for documenting sources in research-based English papers is the MLA (Modern Language Association) system described here.

- All sources are briefly mentioned by author name in the text.

- A list of Works Cited at the end lists full publication data for each source named in the paper.

- Additional explanatory information written by the writer of the paper can be included in footnotes or endnotes.

The MLA documentation system is explained in authoritative detail in the *MLA Handbook for Writers of Research Papers*, 6th ed. (New York: MLA, 2003), or on the MLA Web site <*http://www.mla.org*>.

## 53  Guidelines for Formatting Manuscripts

The MLA guidelines for submitting college papers are fairly conservative and do not reflect the wealth of visually interesting options in fonts, point sizes, visual insertions, and other features available on most modern word processors. If your instructor requests MLA format, follow the guidelines here. If your instructor encourages more open journalistic formats, use good judgment in displaying the information in your text.

### Paper and printing

Print all academic assignments on clean white 8½-by-11-inch paper in a standard font (e.g., Times New Roman, Courier) and point size (11–12) using a good-quality printer.

### Margins and spacing

Allow margins of one inch all around. Justify the left margin only. Double-space everything, including headings, quoted material, and the Works Cited page. Indent the first line of each paragraph five spaces or one-half inch. Indent every line of a prose quotation of more than four lines or poetry of more than three lines twice as far—ten spaces or one inch. (Do not use quotation marks when quotations are displayed in this way.)

### Identification

On page 1, include your name, instructor's name, course title, and the date on separate lines, double-spaced, flush with the upper left margin. Double-space to the title.

### Title

Center the title on the first page using conventional title case punctuation (capitalizing key words only). If your instructor asks for strict MLA style, avoid using italics, underlining, quotation marks, boldface, unusual fonts, or an enlarged point size for the title. (MLA does not require a title page or an outline.) Double-space to the first paragraph.

## Page numbers

Set page numbers to print in the upper right margin of all pages, one-half inch below the top of the paper. If following strict MLA form, include your last name before each page number to guarantee correct identification of stray pages (Turner 1, Turner 2, etc.).

## Punctuation

Use one space after commas, semicolons, colons, periods, question marks, exclamation points, and between the periods in an ellipsis. Dashes are formed by two hyphens, with no extra spacing on either side.

## Visual information

Label each table or chart as Table 1, Table 2, and so on. Label each drawing or photograph as Figure 1 (or Fig. 1), Figure 2, and so on. Include a clear caption for each, and place in the text as near as possible to the passage that refers to it.

# 54   Guidelines for In-Text Citations

The following guidelines explain how to include research sources in the main body of your text using MLA style.

## 54a. Citing sources in the text

Each source mentioned in your paper needs to be accompanied by a brief citation consisting of the author's last name and the page number. These are placed either in the text itself or in parentheses following the cited material. This **in-text citation** refers readers to the alphabetical list of Works Cited at the paper's end, which gives full publication information about each source.

## 1. Author identified in a signal phrase

When you include the source author's name in the sentence introducing the source, add only the specific page on which the material appeared in parentheses following the information.

> Carol Lea Clark explains the basic necessities for the creation of a page on the World Wide Web (77).

Do not include the word *page* or the abbreviation *p.* before the number; the parenthetical reference comes before the period.

For a work by *two or three authors,* include all authors' names:

> Clark and Jones explain . . .

For works with *more than three authors,* list all authors or use the first author's name and add *et al.* (Latin abbreviation for "and others") without a comma:

> Britton et al. suggest . . .

## 2. Author not identified in a signal phrase

If you do not mention the author's name in your text, add it in the parentheses just before the source page number. Do not punctuate between the author's name and the page number.

> Provided one has certain "basic ingredients," the Web offers potential worldwide publication (Clark 77).

For a work by two or three authors, include all authors' last names:

> (Clark and Jones 15)
>
> (Smith, Web, and Beck 210).

For works with more than three authors, list all authors' last names or list the first author only, adding *et al.*

> (White et al. 95)

## 3. Two or more works by the same author

Each citation needs to identify the specific work. If there are two or more works by the same author on your Works Cited list, you must indicate which work is being cited. Either mention the title of the work in the text, or include a shortened version of the title (usually the first one or two important words) in the parenthetical citation. Here are three correct ways to do this:

> According to Lewis Thomas in *Lives of a Cell*, many bacteria become dangerous only if they manufacture exotoxins (76).

> According to Lewis Thomas, many bacteria become dangerous only if they manufacture exotoxins (*Lives* 76).

> Many bacteria become dangerous only if they manufacture exotoxins (Thomas, *Lives* 76).

Identify the shortened title by underlining (e.g., published titles) or quotation marks (e.g., articles), as appropriate.

## 4. Unknown author

When the author of a work is unknown, either give the complete title in the text or a shortened version in the parenthetical citation, along with the page number.

> According to *Statistical Abstracts,* in 1990 the literacy rate for Mexico stood at 75% (374).

> In 1990 the literacy rate for Mexico stood at 75% (*Statistical* 374).

## 5. Corporate or organizational author

Indicate the group's full name in either text or parentheses:

> (Florida League of Women Voters 3)

If the name is long, it is best to cite it in the text sentence and put only the page number in parentheses.

## 6. Authors with the same last name

When you cite works by two or more different authors with the same last name, include the first initial of each author's name in the parenthetical citation:

> (C. Miller 63; S. Miller 101-04).

## 7. Works in more than one volume

Indicate the pertinent volume number for each citation before the page number, and follow it with a colon and one space:

> (Hill 2: 70)

If your source is one volume of a multivolume work, do not specify the volume number in your text, but specify it in the Works Cited list.

## 8. One-page works

When you refer to a work that is one page long, do not include the page number because it will appear in the Works Cited list.

## 9. Quotation from a secondary source

When a quotation or any information in your source is originally from another source, use the abbreviation *qtd. in.*

> Lester Brown of Worldwatch feels that international agricultural production has reached its limit (qtd. in Mann 51).

## 10. Poem or play

In citing poems, name part (if divided into parts) and line numbers; include the word *line* or *lines* in the first such reference.

> In "The Mother," Gwendolyn Brooks remembers "the children you got that you did not get" (line 1).

When you cite up to three lines from a poem in your text, separate the lines with a slash with a space before and after it.

> Emily Dickinson describes being alive in a New England summer: "Inebriate of air am I / And debauchee of dew / Reeling through endless summer days" (lines 6-8).

When you cite more than three lines, indent each line ten spaces or one inch (see item 12).

Cite plays using act, scene, and (for verse plays) line numbers, separated by periods. For major works such as *Hamlet,* use identifiable abbreviations.

> (Ibsen 2.2)      (Ham. 4.4.31.39)

## 11. More than one work in a citation

To cite two or more works, separate them with semicolons.

(Aronson, *Golden Shore* 177; Didion 49-50)

## 12. Long quotation set off from text

To set off quoted passages of five or more lines, indent ten spaces or one inch from the left-hand margin of the text (not from the paper's edge); double-space, and omit quotation marks. The parenthetical citation *follows* end punctuation (unlike citations for shorter, integrated quotations) and is not followed by a period.

> Fellow author W. Somerset Maugham had this to say about Austen's dialogue:
>
> > No one has ever looked upon Jane Austen as a great stylist. Her spelling was peculiar and her grammar often shaky, but she had a good ear. Her dialogue is probably as natural as dialogue can ever be. To set down on paper speech as it is spoken would be very tedious, and some arrangement of it is necessary. (434)

## 13. Electronic texts

The MLA guidelines on documenting electronic sources are explained in detail online at <*http://www.mla.org/set_stl.htm*>.

Electronic sources are cited in the body of the text the same as print sources: by author, title of text, or title of Web site and page numbers. If no page numbers appear on the source, include section (sec.) number or title and/or paragraph (par.) numbers.

> The Wizard of Oz "was nominated for six Academy Awards, including Best Picture" (Wizard par. 3).

However, Web pages commonly omit page and section numbers and are not organized by paragraphs. In such cases, omit numbers from your parenthetical references. (For a document downloaded from the Web, the page numbers of a printout should normally not be cited because pagination may vary in different printouts.)

> In the United States, the birth rate per 1,000 people has fallen steadily from 16.7 in 1995 to 12.1 in 2004 (<u>Statistical</u>).

## 54b.  Using notes to provide additional information

MLA style uses notes primarily to offer comments, explanations, or additional information (especially source-related information) that cannot be smoothly or easily accommodated in the text of the paper. In general, however, avoid presenting information outside the main body of your paper, unless it is necessary for clarification or justification. If a note is necessary, insert a raised (superscript) numeral at the reference point in the text. Introduce the note itself with a corresponding raised numeral, and indent it.

**TEXT WITH SUPERSCRIPT**

The standard ingredients for guacamole include avocados, lemon juice, onion, tomatoes, coriander, salt, and pepper.[1] Hurtado's poem, however, gives this traditional dish a whole new twist (lines 10-17).

**NOTE**

> [1]For variations, see Beard 314, Egerton 197, and Eckhardt 92. Beard's version, which includes olives and green peppers, is the most unusual.

Any published references listed in the notes must also appear in the Works Cited list.

Notes may come at the bottom of the page on which the superscript appears, single-spaced, as footnotes, or they may be presented as endnotes, double-spaced, on a separate page at the end of your paper, preceding the Works Cited list, with the title Note or Notes.

# 55    Sample First Page in MLA Style

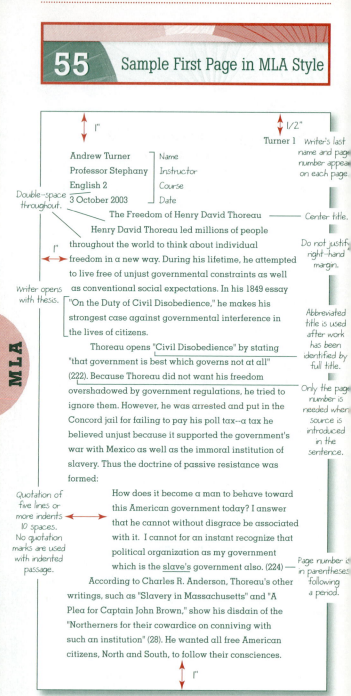

*1"*

*1/2"*

Turner 1    *Writer's last name and page number appear on each page.*

Andrew Turner    } *Name*
Professor Stephany    } *Instructor*
English 2    } *Course*
3 October 2003    } *Date*

*Double-space throughout.*

The Freedom of Henry David Thoreau — *Center title.*

Henry David Thoreau led millions of people throughout the world to think about individual freedom in a new way. During his lifetime, he attempted to live free of unjust governmental constraints as well as conventional social expectations. In his 1849 essay "On the Duty of Civil Disobedience," he makes his strongest case against governmental interference in the lives of citizens.

*1"*

*Writer opens with thesis.*

*Do not justify right-hand margin.*

*Abbreviated title is used after work has been identified by full title.*

Thoreau opens "Civil Disobedience" by stating "that government is best which governs not at all" (222). Because Thoreau did not want his freedom overshadowed by government regulations, he tried to ignore them. However, he was arrested and put in the Concord jail for failing to pay his poll tax--a tax he believed unjust because it supported the government's war with Mexico as well as the immoral institution of slavery. Thus the doctrine of passive resistance was formed:

*Only the page number is needed when source is introduced in the sentence.*

*Quotation of five lines or more indents 10 spaces. No quotation marks are used with indented passage.*

How does it become a man to behave toward this American government today? I answer that he cannot without disgrace be associated with it. I cannot for an instant recognize that political organization as my government which is the slave's government also. (224) —

According to Charles R. Anderson, Thoreau's other writings, such as "Slavery in Massachusetts" and "A Plea for Captain John Brown," show his disdain of the "Northerners for their cowardice on conniving with such an institution" (28). He wanted all free American citizens, North and South, to follow their consciences.

*Page number is in parentheses following a period.*

*1"*

*MLA*

*Sample First Page of a Student Essay in MLA Format*

# 56 Guidelines for the MLA Works Cited Page

Identify every source mentioned in the body of your paper in a Works Cited list attached to the end of the paper using the following format.

- Center the title Works Cited, with no quotation marks, underlining, or boldface, one inch from the top of a separate page following the final page of the paper.

- Number this page, following in sequence from the last numbered page of your paper. If the list runs more than a page, continue the page numbering in sequence, but do not repeat the Works Cited title.

- Double-space between the title and first entry and within and between entries.

- Begin each entry at the left-hand margin, and indent subsequent lines the equivalent of a paragraph indention (five spaces or one-half inch).

## 56a. Order of entries

Alphabetize entries according to authors' last names. If an author is unknown, alphabetize according to the first word of the title, ignoring an initial *A, An,* or *The.*

### Entry formats

Each item in the entry begins with a capital letter and is followed by a period. Each period is followed by one space. Capitalize all major words in the book and article titles. Underline published titles (books, periodicals); put quotation marks around chapters, articles, stories, and poems within published works. Do not underline volume and issue numbers or end punctuation. The four most common variations on general formats are the following:

**BOOKS**

Author(s). <u>Book Title</u>. Place of publication: Publisher, year of publication.

**JOURNAL ARTICLES**

Author(s). "Article Title." <u>Journal Title</u> volume (year of publication): inclusive page numbers.

### MAGAZINE AND NEWSPAPER ARTICLES

Author(s). "Article Title." <u>Publication Title</u> date of
    publication: inclusive page numbers.

### ELECTRONIC SOURCES

Author(s). "Document Title." <u>Published Source Title</u>.
    Date of publication: number of pages,
    sections, or paragraphs. Sponsoring
    organization. Date of access <electronic
    address>.

#### AUTHORS

- List the author's last name first, followed by a comma and then the rest of the name as it appears on the publication, followed by a period. Never alter an author's name by replacing full spellings with initials or by dropping middle initials.

- For more than one author, use a comma rather than a period after the first author; list the other authors' full names, first name first, separated by commas. Do not use an ampersand (&). Put a period at the end.

- For more than one work by the same author, use three hyphens for the name after the first entry.

#### TITLES

- List full titles and subtitles as they appear on the title page of a book or in the credits for a film, video, or recording. Separate titles and subtitles with colons (followed by one space).

- Underline titles of entire books and periodicals.

- Use quotation marks around the titles of essays, poems, songs, short stories, and other parts of a larger work.

- Put a period after a book or article title. Use no punctuation after a journal, magazine, or newspaper title.

#### PLACES OF PUBLICATION

- Places of publication are given for books and pamphlets, not for journals or magazines.

- Give the city of publication from the title page or copyright page. If several cities are given, use only the first.

- For a city outside the United States that might be unfamiliar to your reader, abbreviate the name of the country or Canadian province, preceded by a comma.

- Use a colon to separate the place of publication from the publisher.

- For electronic sources, include the Internet address at the end of the entry in angle brackets.

### PUBLISHERS

- The name of the publisher is given for books and pamphlets.

- Shorten the publisher's name as described under Abbreviations on page 152. If a title page indicates both an imprint and a publisher (for example, Arbor House, an imprint of William Morrow), list both shortened names, separated by a hyphen (Arbor-Morrow).

- Use a comma to separate the publisher from the publication date.

### DATE

- For books, give the year of publication followed by a period.

- For journals, give the year of publication within parentheses followed by a colon.

- For magazines and newspapers, put a colon after the date.

- For newspapers, put the day before the month and year (25 May 1954) with no commas separating the elements.

- For electronic sources, include the date the site was accessed.

### PAGE NUMBERS

- Page numbers are included for all publications other than books.

- Use a hyphen, not a dash, between inclusive page numbers, with no extra space on either side (52-55).

- Use all digits for ending page numbers up to 99 and the last two digits only for numbers above 99 (130-38) unless the full number is needed for clarity (198-210).

**MLA**

- If subsequent pages do not follow consecutively, use a plus sign after the last consecutive page number (39; 50–52+).

- If no page numbers are available for electronic sources, include paragraph or section numbers.

### ABBREVIATIONS

- To shorten a publisher's name, drop the words *Press, Company,* and so forth, in the publisher's name (Blair for Blair Press). Use the abbreviation UP for University Press (Columbia UP; U of Chicago P).

- If the publisher's name is a series of names, use only the first name (Farrar for Farrar, Straus & Giroux). Use only the last name if the publisher's name is a person's name (Abrams for Harry N. Abrams).

- If no publisher or date of publication is given for a source, use the abbreviations *n.p.* (no publisher) or *n.d.* (no date).

- For periodicals, abbreviate months using the first three letters followed by a period (Apr., Dec.) except for September (Sept.); do not abbreviate May, June, and July. If an issue covers two months, use a hyphen to connect the months (Apr.–May, June–Aug.).

## 56b.  Documenting books

### 1. BOOK BY ONE AUTHOR

Thomas, Lewis. Lives of a Cell: Notes of a Biology Watcher. New York: Viking, 1974.

### 2. BOOK BY TWO OR THREE AUTHORS

Fulwiler, Toby, and Alan R. Hayakawa. The Blair Handbook. Boston: Blair-Prentice, 1994.

Second and third authors are listed first name first. Do not alphabetize the author's names within an individual Works Cited entry. The final author's name is preceded by *and*. Do not use an ampersand (&). A comma always follows the inverted ordering of the author's first name.

### 3. BOOK BY MORE THAN THREE AUTHORS

Britton, James, et al. The Development of Writing Abilities. London: Macmillan, 1975.

With more than three authors, you have the option of using the abbreviation *et al.* ("and others") or listing all the authors' names in full as they appear on the title page of the book. Do not alphabetize the names within the Works Cited entry.

### 4. BOOK BY A CORPORATION, ORGANIZATION, OR ASSOCIATION

US Coast Guard Auxiliary. <u>Boating Skills and Seamanship</u>. Washington: Coast Guard Aux. Natl. Board, 1997.

Alphabetize by the name of the organization.

### 5. REVISED EDITION OF A BOOK

Hayakawa, S. I. <u>Language in Thought and Action</u>. 4th ed. New York: Harcourt, 1978.

### 6. EDITED BOOK

Hoy, Pat C., II, Esther H. Shor, and Robert Di Yanni, eds. <u>Women's Voices: Visions and Perspectives</u>. New York: McGraw, 1990.

### 7. BOOK WITH AN EDITOR AND AN AUTHOR

Britton, James. <u>Prospect and Retrospect</u>. Ed. Gordon Pradl. Upper Montclair: Boynton, 1982.

The abbreviation *Ed.* followed by a name replaces the phrase "edited by" and cannot be made plural. (See models 13 and 14.)

### 8. BOOK IN MORE THAN ONE VOLUME

Waldrep, Tom, ed. <u>Writers on Writing</u>. 2 vols. New York: Random, 1985-88.

When separate volumes were published in different years, use inclusive dates.

### 9. ONE VOLUME OF A MULTIVOLUME BOOK

Waldrep, Tom, ed. <u>Writers on Writing</u>. Vol. 2. New York: Random, 1988.

When each volume has its own title, list the full publication information for the volume you have used first, followed by information on the series (number of volumes, dates).

Churchill, Winston S. <u>Triumph and Tragedy</u>. Boston: Houghton, 1953. Vol. 6 of <u>The Second World War</u>. 6 vols. 1948-53.

**MLA**

### 10. TRANSLATED BOOK

Camus, Albert. <u>The Stranger</u>. Trans. Stuart Gilbert.
    New York: Random, 1946.

### 11. BOOK IN A SERIES

Magistrate, Anthony. <u>Stephen King, the Second</u>
    <u>Decade</u>: Danse Macabre <u>to</u> The Dark Half.
    Twayne Amer. Authors Ser. 599. New York:
    Twayne, 1992.

A book title appearing in a book's title is not underlined
(or italicized). Add series information just before city of
publication.

### 12. REPRINTED BOOK

Hurston, Zora Neale. <u>Their Eyes Were Watching</u>
    <u>God</u>. 1937. New York: Perennial-Harper, 1990.

Add the original publication date after the title, and then
cite current edition information.

### 13. INTRODUCTION, PREFACE, FOREWORD, OR AFTERWORD IN A BOOK

Selfe, Cynthia. Foreword. <u>Electronic</u>
    <u>Communication across the Curriculum</u>.
    Ed. Donna Rice et al. Urbana: NCTE,
    1998. ix-xiv.

### 14. WORK IN AN ANTHOLOGY OR CHAPTER IN AN EDITED COLLECTION

Donne, John. "The Canonization." <u>The Metaphysical</u>
    <u>Poets</u>. Ed. Helen Gardner. Baltimore: Penguin,
    1957. 61-62.

Use quotation marks around the title of the work (poem,
short story, essay, chapter) unless the work was originally
published as a book. In that case, underline (or italicize)
the title. Add inclusive page numbers for the selection at the
end of the entry.

### 15. ESSAY OR PERIODICAL ARTICLE REPRINTED IN A COLLECTION

Emig, Janet. "Writing as Mode of Learning." <u>College</u>
    <u>Composition and Communication</u> 28 (1977):
    122-28. Rpt. in <u>The Web of Meaning</u>. Ed. Janet
    Emig. Upper Montclair: Boynton, 1983. 123-31.

Include the full citation for the original publication, followed by *Rpt. in* (Reprinted in) and the publication

information for the book. Give inclusive page numbers for the article or essay found in the collection; add inclusive page numbers for the original source when available.

### 16. ARTICLES IN A REFERENCE BOOK

"Behn, Aphra." <u>The Concise Columbia Encyclopedia</u>. 1998 ed.

### 17. ANONYMOUS BOOK

<u>The World Almanac and Book of Facts</u>. New York: World Almanac-Funk, 2000.

Alphabetize by title, excluding an initial *A, An,* or *The.*

### 18. GOVERNMENT DOCUMENT

United States. Central Intelligence Agency. <u>National Basic Intelligence Fact Book</u>. Washington: GPO, 1999.

If the author is identified, begin with that name. If not, begin with the government (country or state), followed by the agency or organization. The US Government Printing Office is abbreviated GPO.

### 19. DISSERTATION

Kitzhaber, Albert R. "Rhetoric in American Colleges." Diss. U of Washington, 1953.

Use quotation marks for the title of an unpublished dissertation. Include the university name and the year. For a published dissertation, underline (or italicize) the title and give publication information as you would for a book, including the order number if the publisher is University Microfilms International (UMI).

## 56c. Documenting periodicals

### 20. ARTICLE, STORY, OR POEM IN A MONTHLY OR BIMONTHLY MAGAZINE

"From Beans to Brew." <u>Consumer Reports</u> Nov. 1999: 43-46.

Abbreviate all months except May, June, and July. Hyphenate months for bimonthlies (July–Aug. 2003). Do not list volume or issue numbers. For an unsigned article, alphabetize by title.

MLA

**MLA**

### 21. ARTICLE, STORY, OR POEM IN A WEEKLY MAGAZINE

Ross, Alex. "The Wanderer." New Yorker 10 May
    1999: 56-63.

Note that when the day of the month is specified, the publication date is inverted.

### 22. ARTICLE IN A DAILY NEWSPAPER

Brody, Jane E. "Doctors Get Poor Marks for Nutrition
    Knowledge." New York Times 10 Feb. 1992: B7.

For an unsigned article, alphabetize by the title. Give the full name of the newspaper as it appears on the masthead, but drop an introductory *A, An,* or *The.*

If the city is not in the name, it should follow in brackets: *El Diario* [Los Angeles].

With the page number, include the letter that designates any separately numbered sections. If sections are numbered consecutively, list the section number (sec. 2) before the colon, preceded by a comma.

### 23. ARTICLE IN A JOURNAL PAGINATED BY VOLUME

Harris, Joseph. "The Other Reader." Journal of
    Advanced Composition 12 (1992): 34-36.

If the page numbers are continuous from one issue to the next throughout the year, include only the volume number (always in Arabic numerals) and year. Do not give the issue number or month or season. Note that there is no space between the closing parenthesis and the colon.

### 24. ARTICLE IN A JOURNAL PAGINATED BY ISSUE

Tiffin, Helen. "Post-Colonialism, Post-Modernism,
    and the Rehabilitation of Post-Colonial
    History." Journal of Commonwealth
    Literature 23.1 (1998): 169-81.

If each issue begins with page 1, include the volume number followed by a period and then the issue number (both in Arabic numerals, even if the journal uses Roman). Do not give the month of publication.

### 25. EDITORIAL

"Gay Partnership Legislation a Mixed Bag."
    Editorial. Burlington Free Press 5 Apr. 2000:
    A10.

If an editorial is signed, list the author's name first.

### 26. LETTER TO THE EDITOR AND REPLY

Kempthorne, Charles. Letter. Kansas City Star
26 July 1999: A16.

Massing, Michael. Reply to letter of Peter Dale Scott.
New York Review of Books 4 Mar. 1993: 57.

### 27. REVIEW

Kramer, Mimi. "Victims." Rev. of 'Tis Pity She's a
Whore. New York Shakespeare Festival. New
Yorker 20 Apr. 1992: 78-79.

## 56d. Documenting electronic sources

Electronic sources include both databases, available in portable forms such as CD–ROM, diskette, or magnetic tape, and online sources accessed with a computer connected to the Internet.

### Databases

The Works Cited entries for electronic databases (newsletters, journals, and conferences) are similar to entries for articles in printed periodicals.

### 28. PERIODICALLY UPDATED CD-ROM DATABASE

James, Caryn. "An Army as Strong as Its Weakest
Link." New York Times 16 Sept. 1994: C8. New
York Times Ondisc. CD-ROM. UMI-ProQuest.
Oct. 1994.

If a database comes from a printed source such as a book, periodical, or collection of bibliographies or abstracts, cite this information first, followed by the title of the database (underlined), the medium of publication, the vendor name (if applicable), and the date of electronic publication. If no printed source is available, include the title of the material accessed (in quotation marks), the date of the material if given, the underlined title of the database, the medium of publication, the vendor name, and the date of electronic publication.

### 29. NONPERIODICAL CD-ROM PUBLICATION

"Rhetoric." The Oxford English Dictionary. 2nd ed.
CD-ROM. Oxford: Oxford UP, 1992.

List a nonperiodical CD–ROM as you would a book, adding the medium of publication and information about the source, if applicable. If citing only part of a work, underline the title of the selected portion or place it within quotation marks, as appropriate.

**30. DISKETTE OR MAGNETIC TAPE PUBLICATION**

Lanham, Richard D. <u>The Electronic Word:</u>
<u>Democracy, Technology, and the Arts.</u>
Diskette. Chicago: U of Chicago P, 1993.

## Online sources

Documenting a World Wide Web (WWW) or other Internet source follows the same basic guidelines as documenting other texts: Indicate *who said what, where, and when.* However, there are some important differences. When you cite online sources from the Web or electronic mail (e-mail), two dates are important: the date the text was created (published) and the date you found the information (accessed the site). When both publication and access dates are available, provide both.

However, many WWW sources are often updated or changed, leaving no trace of the original version, so always provide the access date, which documents that this information was available on that particular date. Therefore, most electronic source entries will end with an access date immediately followed by the electronic address: 23 Dec. 2003 <http://www.cas.usf.edu/english>. The angle brackets < > identify the source as the Internet.

The following guidelines are derived from the MLA Web site *<http://www.mla.org>*. To identify a WWW or Internet source, include, if available, the following items in the following order, each punctuated by a period, except date of access:

- **Author (or else editor, compiler, or translator).** If known, use full name, last name first.

- **Title.** Put the titles of poems, short stories, and articles in quotation marks. Put the title of a posting to a discussion list or forum in quotation marks followed by *Online posting.*

- **Editor, compiler, or translator.** If not cited earlier, include name here, preceded by the appropriate abbreviation (*Ed., Comp., Trans.*).

- **Print source.** Include the same information as in a printed citation.

- **Title** of scholarly project, database, personal, or professional site (underlined); if there is no title, include a description such as *Home page.*
- **Identifying number.** For a journal, include volume and issue number.
- **Date of electronic publication.**
- **Discussion list** information. Include full name or title of list or forum.
- **Page, paragraph, or section numbers.**
- **Sponsorship or affiliation.** Include the name of any organization or institution sponsoring the site.
- **Date of access.** This is the date you visited the site.
- **Electronic address.** Place within angle brackets < >.

### 31. PUBLISHED WEB SITE

Beller, Jonathon L. "What's Inside The Insider?" Pop
Matters Film. 1999. 21 May 2000 <http://
popmatters.com/film/insider.html>.

### 32. PERSONAL WEB SITE

Fulwiler, Toby. Home page. 2 Apr. 2004 <http://
www.uvm.edu/~tfulwile>.

### 33. PROFESSIONAL WEB SITE

Yellow Wallpaper Site. 1995. U of Texas. 4 Mar. 1998
<http://www.cwrl.utexas.edu/~daniel/
amlit/wallpaper.html>.

### 34. BOOK

Twain, Mark. The Adventures of Tom Sawyer.
Internet Wiretap Online Library. 4 Jan. 1998.
Carnegie Mellon U. 4 Oct. 1998 <http://
www.cs.cmu.edu/Web/People/rgs/
sawyr-table.html>.

To interrupt an electronic address at the end of a line, hit return, but do not hyphenate; break addresses only after a slash.

### 35. POEM

Poe, Edgar Allan. "The Raven." American
Review. 1845. Poetry Archives. 8 Sept. 1998
<http://tqd.advanced.org/3247/cgi-bin/
dispoem.cgi?poet=poe.edgar&poem>.

MLA

**36. ARTICLE IN A JOURNAL**

Erkkila, Betsy. "The Emily Dickinson Wars." <u>Emily Dickinson Journal</u> 5.2 (1996): 14 pars. 8 Nov. 1988 <http://www.colorado.edu/EDIS/journal/index.html>.

**37. ARTICLE IN A REFERENCE DATABASE**

"Victorian." <u>Encyclopaedia Britannica Online</u>. 1997. Encyclopaedia Britannica. 2 Dec. 1997 <http://www.britannica.com>.

**38. POSTING TO A DISCUSSION LIST**

White, Ed. "New York State Mandated Writing Assessment." Online posting. 9 June 2004. WPA: Writing Program Administration, Arizona State U. East. 23 June 2004 <http://lists.asu.edu/archives/wpa-l.html>.

**39. E-MAIL OR LISTSERV**

Fulwiler, Toby. "A Question about Electronic Sources." E-mail to the author. 23 May 2004.

**40. NEWSGROUP (USENET) MESSAGE**

Answerman (Mathes, Robert). "Revising the Atom." Online posting. 2 Mar. 1997. 4 July 1997 <news:alt.books.digest>.

If you quote a personal message sent by somebody else, be sure to get permission before including the person's address on the Works Cited page.

# 56e. Documenting other sources

**41. CARTOON, TITLED OR UNTITLED**

Davis, Jim. "Garfield." Cartoon. <u>Courier</u> [Findlay] 17 Feb. 1996: E4.

**42. FILM OR VIDEOCASSETTE**

<u>Casablanca</u>. Dir. Michael Curtiz. Perf. Humphrey Bogart and Ingrid Bergman. Warner Bros., 1942.

<u>Fast Food: What's in It for You</u>. Prod. Center for Science. Videocassette. Los Angeles: Churchill, 1988.

Begin with the title, followed by the director, the studio, and the year released. You may also include the names of lead actors, producer, and the like, between the title and the distribution information. If your essay is concerned with a particular person's work on a film, lead with that person's name, arranging all other information accordingly.

> Lewis, Joseph H., dir. Gun Crazy. Screenplay by
> Dalton Trumbo. King Bros., 1950.

#### 43. PERSONAL INTERVIEW

> Holden, James. Personal interview. 12 Jan. 2000.

Begin with the interviewee's name, and specify the kind of interview and the date. You may identify the interviewee's position if it is relevant to the purpose of the interview.

> Morser, John. Professor of Political Science, U of
> Wisconsin--Stevens Point. Telephone
> interview. 15 Dec. 2002.

#### 44. PUBLISHED OR BROADCAST INTERVIEW

> Steingass, David. Interview. Counterpoint 7 May
> 1970: 3-4.

For published or broadcast interviews, begin with the interviewee's name. Include appropriate publication information for a periodical or book and appropriate broadcast information for a radio or television program.

#### 45. PRINT ADVERTISEMENT

> Cadillac De Ville. Advertisement. New York Times
> 21 Feb. 1996, natl. ed.: A20.

Begin with the name of the product, followed by the description *Advertisement* and publication information for the source.

#### 46. UNPUBLISHED LECTURE, PUBLIC ADDRESS, OR SPEECH

> Graves, Donald. "When Bad Things Happen to Good
> Ideas." National Council of Teachers of
> English Convention. St. Louis. 21 Nov. 1989.

Begin with the speaker, followed by the title (if any), the meeting (and sponsoring organization, if needed), the location, and the date. If there is no title, use a descriptive label (such as *Speech*) with no quotation marks.

### 47. PERSONAL OR UNPUBLISHED LETTER

Friedman, Paul. Letter to the author. 18 Mar. 2003.

Personal letters and e-mail messages are handled nearly identically in Works Cited entries. Begin with the name of the writer, identify the type of communication (e.g., *Letter*), and specify the audience. Include the date written, if known, or the date received.

To cite an unpublished letter from an archive or private collection, include information that locates the holding (for example, Quinn-Adams Papers. Lexington Historical Society, Lexington).

### 48. PUBLISHED LETTER

King, Martin Luther, Jr. "Letter from Birmingham Jail." 28 Aug. 1963. <u>Civil Disobedience in Focus</u>. Ed. Hugo Adam Bedau. New York: Routledge, 1991. 68-84.

Cite published letters as you would a selection from an anthology. Specify the audience in the letter title (if known). Include the date of the letter immediately after its title. Place the page number or range after the publisher information. If you cite more than one letter from a collection, cite the entire collection in the Works Cited list, and indicate individual dates and page numbers in your text.

### 49. MAP

<u>Ohio River: Foster, KY, to New Martinsville, WV</u>. Map. Huntington: US Army Corps of Engineers, 1985.

Cite a map as you would a book by an unknown author. Underline the title and identify the source as a map or chart.

### 50. PERFORMANCE

Bissex, Rachel, perf. <u>Let Me Sing for You</u>. Flynn Theater, Burlington. 14 May 1990.

Identify the pertinent details, such as title, place, and date of the performance. If you focus on a particular person in your essay, such as the director or conductor, lead with that person's name. For a recital or individual concert, lead with the performer's name.

### 51. AUDIO RECORDING

Marley, Bob, and the Wailers. "Buffalo Soldier." <u>Legend</u>. Audiocassette. Island Records, 1984.

Depending on the focus of your essay, begin with the artist, composer, or conductor. Enclose song titles in quotation marks, followed by the recording title, underlined. Do not underline musical compositions identified only by form, number, and key. If you are not citing a compact disc, specify the recording format. End with the company label, the catalog number (if known), and the date of issue.

### 52. TELEVISION OR RADIO BROADCAST

"Emissary." <u>Star Trek: Deep Space Nine</u>. Teleplay by
Michael Pillar. Story by Rick Berman and
Michael Pillar. Dir. David Carson. Fox. WFLX,
West Palm Beach. 9 Jan. 1993.

If the broadcast is not an episode of a series or the episode is untitled, begin with the program title. Include the network, the station and city, and the date of broadcast.

### 53. WORK OF ART

Holbein, Hans. <u>Portrait of Erasmus</u>. Louvre, Paris.
<u>The Louvre Museum</u>. By Germain Bazin. New
York: Abrams, n.d. 148.

Begin with the artist's name. Follow with the title, and conclude with the location. If your source is a book, also give pertinent publication information.

**MLA**

# 57 Sample Works Cited Page in MLA Style

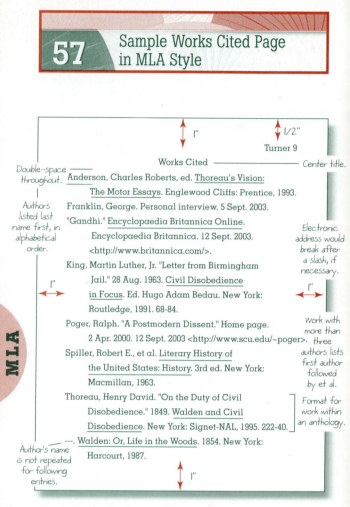

1"  1/2"

Turner 9

Works Cited — Center title.

Double-space throughout.

Anderson, Charles Roberts, ed. <u>Thoreau's Vision:</u>
  <u>The Motor Essays</u>. Englewood Cliffs: Prentice, 1993.

Authors listed last name first, in alphabetical order.

Franklin, George. Personal interview. 5 Sept. 2003.

"Gandhi." <u>Encyclopædia Britannica Online</u>.
  Encyclopædia Britannica. 12 Sept. 2003.
  <http://www.britannica.com/>.

Electronic address would break after a slash, if necessary.

King, Martin Luther, Jr. "Letter from Birmingham
  Jail." 28 Aug. 1963. <u>Civil Disobedience
  in Focus</u>. Ed. Hugo Adam Bedau. New York:
  Routledge, 1991. 68-84.

1"   1"

Poger, Ralph. "A Postmodern Dissent." Home page.
  2 Apr. 2000. 12 Sept. 2003 <http://www.scu.edu/~poger>.

Work with more than three authors lists first author followed by et al.

Spiller, Robert E., et al. <u>Literary History of
  the United States: History</u>. 3rd ed. New York:
  Macmillan, 1963.

Thoreau, Henry David. "On the Duty of Civil
  Disobedience." 1849. <u>Walden and Civil
  Disobedience</u>. New York: Signet-NAL, 1995. 222-40.

Format for work within an anthology.

Author's name is not repeated for following entries.

---. <u>Walden: Or, Life in the Woods</u>. 1854. New York:
  Harcourt, 1987.

1"

*Sample Works Cited Page of a Student Essay in MLA Format*

MLA

# APA Documentation

Most disciplines in the social sciences and related fields use the name-and-date system of documentation put forth by the American Psychological Association (APA). The disciplines of education and business also use this system. This citation style highlights dates of publication because the currency of published material is of primary importance in these disciplines. Because collaborative authoring is common in the social sciences, listing the first six authors fully in the References is the current standard. For more about the foundations and purposes of the APA system, see the *Publication Manual of the American Psychological Association,* 5th ed. (Washington: APA, 2001) or the APA Web page *<http://www.apa.org/>*.

# 58 Guidelines for Formatting Manuscripts

The APA *Publication Manual* integrates the widespread use of word processors for research, writing, and publication in its guidelines for professionals as well as students. The current standards permit the scholarly use of the special typeface and character options available on most word processors, thus bringing the college writing standards more in line with professional publications. This means that italic typeface rather than underlining is recommended for titles, emphasis, and so on. You will also note other standard publishing features in the models, such as the solid long (or em) dash instead of two hyphens. However, the *Manual* recommends caution: Overuse of font size or design options is never appropriate. Use good judgment, and always ask your instructor about any style or information display preferences he or she requires.

## Paper and printing

Print all academic assignments on clean white 8½-by-11-inch paper in a standard serif font (e.g., Times New Roman, Courier) and point size (11–12) using a good-quality printer.

## Margins and spacing

Allow margins of one inch all around. Justify the left margin only. Double-space everything, including headings, quoted material, and the References page. Indent the first line of each paragraph five spaces or one-half inch.

For prose quotations of more than forty words, indent each line five spaces or one-half inch from the left margin. Do not use quotation marks to mark the beginning and end of displayed quoted passages. Page numbers in parentheses are placed at the end of the passage, following ending punctuation. (*pp. 34–41*).

## Page numbers

Set page numbers to print in the upper right margin of all pages one-half inch below the top of the paper (including title page and abstract). APA format requires a shortened title (two to three words) five spaces before each page number to guarantee correct identification of stray pages (*Green Is 1, Green Is 2,* etc.).

## Title page

Page 1 of an APA-style paper is the title page. Center the title fifteen lines from the top; immediately below, type your name, the course name, your instructor's name, and the date, all centered. Use conventional title case punctuation (capitalizing key words only). Avoid using italics, underlining, quotation marks, boldface, unusual fonts, or an enlarged point size for the title.

## Abstract

Page 2 is the abstract page. Center the word *Abstract* one inch from the top of the page; double-space to the abstract text and throughout. Write a 75- to 100-word (never exceed 120 words) paragraph that states your thesis and the main supporting points in clear, concise, descriptive language. Avoid statements of personal opinion and inflammatory judgments.

## First page of text

On the page following the abstract, center the title of your paper at the top, double-space to the first line of text, and continue double-spacing throughout.

## Punctuation

Use one space after periods, commas, semicolons, colons, question marks, exclamation points, and between the periods in an ellipsis. Long (em) dashes, with no extra spaces on either side, indicate interruptions within a sentence. Short (en) dashes abbreviate the word *to* in page ranges (*pp. 51–64*).

## Visual information

APA requires the labeling of all tables (charts) and figures (drawings, graphs, photographs, etc.) included in the text. Each is numbered in order as *Table 1* or *Figure 1,* and so on. Include a clear title and caption for each, and place in the text as near as possible to the passage it refers to. In your text, be sure to discuss or identify the most important information or feature in each table or figure included.

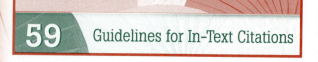

# 59    Guidelines for In-Text Citations

The following guidelines illustrate how to cite reference material in the main body of your paper.

## 1. Single work by one or more authors

Whenever you quote, paraphrase, or summarize material in your text, give both the author's last name and the date of the source. For direct quotations, always provide specific page numbers; for paraphrases, page citations are not required but are a good idea. Page references in the APA system are always preceded, in text or in the reference list (except for journal articles), by the abbreviation *p.* or *pp.* to designate *page* or *pages.*

Supply authors' names, publication dates, and page numbers (when listed) in parentheses following the cited material. Do not repeat any of these elements if you identify them in the text preceding the parenthetical citation.

> Exotoxins make some bacteria dangerous to humans (Thomas, 1974).

> According to Thomas (1974), "Some bacteria are harmful to us only if they make exotoxins" (p. 76).

> We need fear some bacteria only "if they make exotoxins" (Thomas, 1974, p. 76).

For a work by two authors, cite both names.

> Smith and Rogers (1990) agree that all bacteria producing exotoxins are harmful to humans.

> All known exotoxin-producing bacteria are harmful to humans (Smith & Rogers, 1990).

The authors' names are joined by *and* in the text, but APA convention requires an ampersand (&) to join authors' names in parentheses and on the References page.

For a work by three to five authors, identify all the authors by last name the first time you cite a source. In subsequent references, identify only the first author followed by *et al.* ("and others").

The most recent study supports the belief that alcohol abuse is on the rise (Dinkins, Dominic, & Smith, 1989).

When homeless people were excluded from the study, the results were the same (Dinkins et al., 1989).

If you are citing a source by six or more authors, identify only the first author in all the in-text references, followed by *et al.* (See Chapter 61 for References page guidelines.)

## 2. Two or more works by the same author(s) published in the same year

To distinguish between two or more works published in the same year by the same author or team of authors, organize the entries alphabetically by title and then assign a lowercase letter (*a, b, c,* etc.) to each, in sequence, immediately after the date. (These letters will appear after the date in the References as well.) If two such works appear in one citation, repeat the year.

(Smith, 1992a, 1992b)

## 3. Unknown author

To cite the work of an unknown author, identify the first two or three words of the entry as listed on the References page. If the words are from the title, enclose them in quotation marks or underline them, as appropriate.

The literacy rate for Mexico was 75% in 1990, up 4% from a decade earlier (*Statistical Abstracts,* 1991).

## 4. Corporate or organizational author

Spell out the name of the authoring agency for a work by a corporation, association, organization, or foundation. If the name can be abbreviated and remain identifiable, you may spell out the full name the first time, with the abbreviation or acronym in brackets immediately after it. For subsequent references, use only the abbreviation.

(American Psychological Association [APA], 1993)

(APA, 2001)

# 5. Authors with the same last name

To avoid confusion in citing two or more authors with the same last name, include each author's initials in every citation.

> (J. M. Clark, 1994)
>
> (C. L. Clark, 1995)

# 6. Quotation from an indirect source

Use the words *as cited in* for quotations or information from your source but originally from another source.

> Lester Brown of Worldwatch believes that international agriculture production has reached its limit and that "we're going to be in trouble on the food front before this decade is out" (as cited in Mann, 1993, p. 51).

# 7. More than one work in a citation

List two or more sources within a single parenthetical citation in the same order in which they appear in your References list. If you refer to two or more works by the same author, list them in chronological order, with the author's name mentioned once and the dates separated by commas.

> (Thomas, 1974, 1979)

List works by different authors in alphabetical order by the author's last name, separated by semicolons.

> (Miller, 1990; Webster & Rose, 1988)

# 8. A Web site

When citing an entire Web site but not a specific document, page, text, or figure from the site, include the Web address in the text or in parentheses.

> To locate information about the University of Vermont faculty, visit the school's Web site (http://www.uvm.edu).

When the name and Web address is included in the text, no References entry is needed.

# 9. Specific information from a Web site

Cite specific information (author, figure, table, paraphrased or quoted passage) from a Web site as you would a print source, by including the brief author-date information in the text or in parentheses, followed by complete information on the References page.

# 10. Setting off a long quotation from text

Start quotations of forty or more words on a new line, and indent the entire block five spaces or one-half inch from the left-hand margin. Indent the first line of the second or any subsequent paragraphs (but not the first paragraph) five additional spaces. Double-space all such quotations, omit quotation marks, and place the parenthetical citation after end punctuation, with no period following the citation.

# 11. Footnotes

Numbered footnotes provide additional information of interest to some readers but also are likely to slow the pace of your text or obscure your point for other readers.

Make footnotes as brief as possible; when the information you wish to add is extensive, present it in an appendix.

Number footnotes consecutively (as they have been in your text), and present them on a page headed by the word *Footnotes* after the References list. Type all footnotes double-spaced, and indent the first line of each as you would a paragraph.

## 60 Sample Pages in APA Style

The research essay "Green Is Only Skin Deep: False Environmental Marketing" by Elizabeth Bone was written in response to an assignment to identify and explain one problem in contemporary American culture. Bone's essay is documented according to the conventions of the American Psychological Association (APA). This sample from it

Abbreviated title.

Green Is     1

Page numbering begins on title page. A shortened title (2 or 3 words) appears 5 spaces to the left of the number.

Title page information is double-spaced, centered on each line, and placed in the top third of the page (drop about 15 lines from the top).

Green Is Only Skin Deep:   ⌐ Title
False Environmental Marketing
Elizabeth Bone    Author
English 1    Course
Professor John Clark    Instructor
December 6, 2004   ⌐ Date

*Sample Title Page of a Student Essay in APA Format*

Abstract is placed on a separate page following the title page.

1"

1/2"

Green Is     2

Abstract ——— Heading is centered.

No paragraph indent.

1"

Abstract summarizes the main points of the paper.

Most Americans consider themselves environmentalists and favor supporting environmentally friendly or "green" companies. However, companies use a number of false advertising practices to mislead the public about their green practices and products by (1) exaggerating claims, (2) masking false practices behind technical terminology, (3) mis-sponsoring green events, (4) not admitting responsibility for real problems, (5) advertising green by association, and (6) solving one problem while creating others. Consumers must be skeptical of all commercial ads and take the time to find out the truth behind advertising.

Double-space throughout.

Abstract points follow the order in the paper.

*Sample Abstract Page of a Student Essay in APA Format*

Title is repeated from title page and centered.

Double-space throughout.

Green Is Only Skin Deep:
False Environmental Marketing

A recent Gallup poll reported that "75% of Americans consider themselves to be environmentalists" (Smith & Quelch, 1993, p. 9). In the same study, nearly half of the respondents said they would be more likely to purchase a product if they perceived it to be environmentally friendly, or "green." According to Smith and Quelch (1993), because green sells, many companies have begun to promote themselves as marketing products that are either environmentally friendly or manufactured from recycled material. Unfortunately, many of these companies care more about appearance than reality.

The use of technical terms can also mislead average consumers. For example, carbon fluoride compounds, called CFCs, are known to be hazardous to the protective layer of ozone that surrounds the earth, so their widespread use in air conditioners is considered an environmental hazard (Decker & Stammer, 1989). Chrysler Corporation advertises that it uses CFC-free refrigerant in its automobile air conditioners to appeal to environmentally concerned consumers ("Ozone Layer," 1994). However, Weisskopf (1992) points out that "the chemical compounds that replace CFCs in their air conditioners pose other environmental hazards that are not mentioned" (pp. 91–92).

Abbreviated title followed by page number on all pages.

Author last names and date are included in text.

Informational thesis at end of first paragraph.

Example of misleading advertising introduced.

APA

*Sample First Page of a Student Essay in APA Format*

includes the title page, abstract, and first page. Ask your instructor if a separate title page and/or an abstract are required for your course.

## 61 Guidelines for the APA References Page

All works mentioned in a paper should be identified on a reference list according to the following general rules of the APA documentation system.

### 61a. Format

After the final page of the paper, title a separate page *References* with no italics, underlining, or quotation marks. Center the title one inch from the top of the page. Number the page in sequence with the last page of the paper.

Double-space throughout—between the title and the first entry as well as between and within entries. Set the first line flush with the left-hand margin.

Indent the second and all subsequent lines of an entry five spaces (or one default tab) from the left margin in a hanging indent. The paragraph indent format, with the first line indented five spaces, is no longer acceptable.

Do not repeat the title *References* when your reference list exceeds one page.

Alphabetize the list of references according to authors' last names, using the first author's last name for works with multiple authors. For entries by an unknown author, alphabetize by the first word of the title, ignoring an initial *A, An,* or *The.*

### Entry format

Each item in the entry begins with a capital letter and ends with a period. Each period is followed by one space. Only the first word and proper nouns are capitalized in book and article titles; all important words are capitalized in the titles of periodicals. Book and periodical titles are italicized, as are journal volume numbers. The three most common general formats follow:

**BOOKS**

Author(s). (Year of publication). *Book title*. City of
publication: Publisher.

**JOURNAL ARTICLES**

Author(s). (Year of publication). Article title. *Journal
Title*, *volume number*, inclusive page numbers.

**MAGAZINE AND NEWSPAPER ARTICLES**

Author(s). (Year, month of publication). Article title.
*Publication Title*, inclusive page numbers.

### AUTHORS

- List the author's last name first, followed by a
  comma and the author's initials (not first name).

- When a work has more than one author, list all
  authors up to and including the sixth in this way,
  separating the names with a comma. Abbreviate
  more than six authors by placing a comma after the
  initials of the sixth author and typing *et al.*

- For multiple authors for a single work, place an ampersand (&) before the last author's name.

- Place a period after the author name(s) (unless the
  last element is *et al.,* which already ends with a
  period).

### TITLES

- List the complete titles and subtitles of books and
  articles, but capitalize only the first word of the title
  and any subtitle, as well as all proper nouns.
  Separate title and subtitle with a colon.

- Italicize the titles of books, magazines, and newspapers, but do not italicize article titles or place
  quotation marks around them. (Substitute underlining when you are not using a word processor that
  produces italics.)

- Place a period after the title unless it already
  ends with a punctuation mark. Make sure the
  punctuation is italicized also.

### PUBLISHERS

- List publishers' names in shortened form, omitting
  words such as *Company* and *Publishers*. Retain
  *Books* and *Press*.

APA

- Spell out the names of university presses and organizations in full.

- For books, use a colon to separate the city of publication from the publisher.

### DATES AND PAGE NUMBERS

- For magazines and newspapers, use commas to separate the year from the month and day, and enclose the publication dates in parentheses: (1954, May 25).

- Separate inclusive page numbers by an en dash (or a hyphen if this character is difficult to produce) with no spaces: 361–375.

- Use all numbers in ranges of pages and dates: 361–375; 1996–1997.

- If an article is continued on pages that are not consecutive, include subsequent page numbers after a comma: *pp. 1, 16.* (Note that *pp.* precedes the page numbers for newspaper articles but not for journal articles.)

### ABBREVIATIONS

- Abbreviate state and country names but not months.

- Use standard postal abbreviations (NY, VT, WI) to identify the state after the city of publication (but omit them for cities well known for publishing: Baltimore, Boston, Chicago, Los Angeles, New York, Philadelphia, and San Francisco).

Following are examples of the References list format for a variety of source types.

## 61b. Documenting books

### 1. BOOK BY ONE AUTHOR

Benjamin, J. (1988). *The bonds of love: Psychoanalysis, feminism, and the problem of domination.* New York: Prometheus.

### 2. BOOK BY TWO OR MORE AUTHORS

Zweigenhaft, R. L., & Domhoff, G. W. (1991). *Blacks in the white establishment? A study of race and class in America.* New Haven, CT: Yale University Press.

For a book by more than six authors, include the first six authors' names in the References list; substitute *et al.* for the names of the authors beyond the sixth.

### 3. MORE THAN ONE BOOK BY THE SAME AUTHOR

List two or more works by the same author (or the same team of authors listed in the same order) chronologically by year, earliest work first. Arrange any such works published in the same year alphabetically by title, placing lowercase letters after the dates. In either case, give full identification of up to six authors for each listing.

> Bandura, A. (1969). *Principles of behavior modification.* New York: Holt, Rinehart, and Winston.

> Bandura, A. (1997). Self-efficacy: The exercise of control. New York: Freeman.

If the same author is named first but listed with different coauthors, alphabetize by the last name of the second author. Works by the first author alone are listed before works with coauthors.

### 4. BOOK BY A CORPORATION, ASSOCIATION, ORGANIZATION, OR FOUNDATION

> American Psychological Association. (2001). *Publication manual of the American Psychological Association* (5th ed.). Washington, DC: Author.

Alphabetize corporate authors by the corporate name, omitting the articles *A, An,* and *The.* When the corporate author is also the publisher, designate the publisher as *Author.*

### 5. REVISED EDITION OF A BOOK

> Peek, S. (1993). *The game inventor's handbook* (Rev. ed.). Cincinnati, OH: Betterway.

### 6. EDITED BOOK

> Schaefer, C. E., & Reid, S. E. (Eds.). (1986). *Game play: Therapeutic use of childhood games.* New York: Wiley.

Place *Ed.* or *Eds.,* capitalized, after the name(s) of the editor(s) of an edited book.

### 7. BOOK IN MORE THAN ONE VOLUME

Waldrep, T. (Ed.). (1985–1988). *Writers on writing*
(Vols. 1–2). New York: Random House.

For a work with volumes published in different years, indicate the range of dates of publication. In citing only one volume of a multivolume work, indicate only the volume cited.

Waldrep, T. (Ed.). (1988). *Writers on writing* (Vol. 2).
New York: Random House.

### 8. TRANSLATED OR REPRINTED BOOK

Freud, S. (1950). *The interpretation of dreams*
(A. A. Brill, Trans.). New York: Modern Library.
(Original work published 1900)

The date of the translation or reprint is in parentheses after the author's name. Place the original publication date in parentheses at the end of the citation, with no period. In the parenthetical citation in your text, include both dates separated by a slash: *(Freud 1900/1950)*.

### 9. CHAPTER OR ARTICLE IN AN EDITED BOOK

Telander, R. (1996). Senseless crimes. In C. I.
Schuster & W. V. Van Pelt (Eds.), *Speculations:
Readings in culture, identity, and values*
(2nd ed., pp. 264–272). Upper Saddle River, NJ:
Prentice Hall.

The chapter or article title is not underlined or in quotation marks. Editors' names are listed in normal reading order (surname last). Inclusive page numbers, in parentheses, follow the book title.

### 10. ANONYMOUS BOOK

*The world almanac and book of facts.* (2000). New
York: World Almanac.

### 11. GOVERNMENT DOCUMENT

U.S. House of Representatives, Committee on
Energy and Commerce. (1986). *Ensuring
access to programming for the backyard
satellite dish owner* (Serial No. 99-127).
Washington, DC: U.S. Government Printing
Office.

For government documents, provide the higher department or governing agency only when the office or agency that created the document is not readily recognizable. If a document number is available, list it in parentheses after the document title. Write out the name of the printing agency in full rather than using the abbreviation *GPO*. (For documents not available from GPO or a document service, cite the publishing agency.)

# 61c. Documenting periodicals

In citing periodical articles, use the same format for listing author names as for books.

### 12. ARTICLE IN A JOURNAL PAGINATED BY VOLUME

Hartley, J. (1991). Psychology, writing, and computers: A review of research. *Visible Language, 25,* 339–375.

If page numbers are continuous throughout volumes in a year, use only the volume number, italicized, following the italicized title of the periodical; do not use the abbreviation *p.* or *pp.*

### 13. ARTICLE IN A JOURNAL PAGINATED BY ISSUE

Lowther, M. A. (1977). Career change in mid-life: Its impact on education. *Innovator, 8*(7), 1, 9–11.

Include the issue number in parentheses if each issue of a journal is paginated separately; do not use the abbreviation *p.* or *pp.*

### 14. MAGAZINE ARTICLE

Garreau, J. (1995, December). Edgier cities. *Wired,* 158–163, 232–234.

For general-circulation magazines, include the year and month (not abbreviated) after the author's name; do not use the abbreviation *p.* or *pp.*

### 15. NEWSPAPER ARTICLE

Finn, P. (1995, September 27). Death of a U-Va. student raises scrutiny of off-campus drinking. *The Washington Post,* pp. D1, D4.

If an author is listed for the article, begin with the author's name, then list the date (spell out the month); follow with the title of the newspaper. If there is a section, combine it with the page or pages, including all continued page numbers, using the abbreviation *p.* or *pp.* Retain *The* if it is part of the newspaper's name.

## 61d. Documenting electronic sources

Formats for documenting electronic media have been changing and will continue to evolve. The 2001 APA *Publication Manual* (5th ed.; see pp. 268–281 especially) and the APA Web page for electronic docmentation (***http://www.apastyle.org/elecref.html***) are the best sources for up-to-date advice on many specific models. APA style recommendations group electronic sources into two categories: (1) sources on the Internet, further divided into two basic types—periodicals (sources published regularly, such as journals, newsletters, and magazines) and nonperiodicals (books, stand-alone documents, reports, brochures, audiovisual media, etc.)—and (2) other electronic sources (databases, e-mail, software, etc.).

The retrieval statement is the key feature of electronic source references. APA style requires accurate, current electronic addresses (URLs) and full, correct names for host sites or databases in the retrieval statement. The retrieval date gives a reader information about when the site was available to you. This general model, which closely follows the conventions for printed sources, shows the correct use of the retrieval statement.

> Author(s). (date of publication). Article or chapter title. *Title of Periodical, volume number* or *Title of book* or Name of Web Site, inclusive page or paragraph numbers. Retrieved Month day, year, from electronic address or Retrieved Month day, year, from Name of Database, Site Host, Project: electronic address (no final period if entry ends with a URL)

There are three variations of the basic electronic model:

- If it is helpful to the reader, name the Web site (e.g., a complex university or government site) after the word *from* and followed by a colon before the URL.

- If you obtained your source from an aggregated database (no matter its form—on CD-ROM, via libary server, via a Web supplier site), provide the correct full name of the database (not italicized) after the word *from* and end the entry with a period.

■ When you are citing the online version of a printed document and the document has not been changed from the print version (lost its pagination or had links and data added, for example), follow the model for a printed document of its kind but add the words *Electronic version* in square brackets after the title and before the period.

## Documenting online sources

### Periodicals

#### 16. ARTICLE WITH A PRINT VERSION IN AN ONLINE JOURNAL

Green, C. D. (1992) Of immortal mythological beasts: Operationalism in psychology [Electronic version]. *Theory and Psychology 2,* 291–320.

#### 17. ARTICLE IN AN ONLINE-ONLY JOURNAL

Kapadia, S. (1995, November). A tribute to Mahatma Gandhi: His views on women and social exchange. *Journal of South Asia Women Studies, 1*(1). Retrieved March 2, 2002, from http://www.shore.net/~india/bin/mfs/01/ jsaws/ issue1/paper1.htm

Follow this model when the journal article accessed online has been altered from its print version in some way (making the online version to that extent unique), when your source is an Internet-only periodical, or when the article was obtained via file transfer protocol (ftp). No period should be set at the end of an electronic address.

### Nonperiodicals

#### 18. DOCUMENT ON A WORLD WIDE WEB (WWW) SITE

Varkentine, B. (2001). *Best of 2001: A year at the video store.* PopMatters Film and Archive. Retrieved March 21, 2002, from http:// popmatters.com/film/features/ best2001-varkentine.html

#### 19. ONLINE DOCUMENT PUBLISHED BY A PRIVATE ORGANIZATION OR GROUP

American Psychiatric Association. (2001, September 20). *Coping with a national tragedy:*

> *Resources, tools, and other links.* Retrieved
> January 6, 2002, from http://psych.org/
> public_info/copydisaster92001.cfm

If the document has no revisions or publication date, insert
the abbreviation *n.d.* in parentheses after the name of the
organization or group.

### 20. DOCUMENT AVAILABLE ON A UNIVERSITY OR PROGRAM WEB SITE

> Peirce, C. S. (1869, November 25). The English
> doctrine of ideas. *Nation, 9,* 461–462. Retrieved
> January 16, 2002, from IUPUI Peirce Edition
> Project Web site: http://www.iupui.edu/
> ~peirce/web/writings/v2/w2/w2_30/
> v2_30x.htm

This example locates a specific item from a complex university project. An online book, report, or data survey can
be cited using this model.

### 21. E-MAIL MESSAGES

> (R. W. Williams, personal communication, January 4,
> 1998)

E-mail messages are treated as personal conversations and
are not listed on the References page. Cite in the text, as
you would personal letters or interviews.

### 22. NEWSGROUP, ELECTRONIC MAILING LIST, OR ELECTRONIC DISCUSSION GROUP

> Trehub, A. (2002, January 28). The conscious access
> hypothesis [Msg. 18]. Message posted to
> University of Houston Psyche Discussion
> Forum: http://listserv.uh.edu/cgi-bin/
> wa?A2= ind0201&L=psyche-b&F=&S=&P=2334

A searchable, aggregated database is a group of resources
stored in an electronic form for simplified, focused electronic access. APA conventions for documenting aggregated
databases, whether they are fixed (a more static format
published on CD-ROM, diskettes, or magnetic tape is un-
alterable until a new version is produced) or online (a dy-
namic format since inputs or changes—updates, additions,
deletions, inserted links, etc.—can be made at any time
by a producer and the information can be carried by a

number of providers) have been unified in the new standards. It is not necessary to document how or in what form you accessed the database (via portable CD-ROM, on a library server, through a Web site supplier), but a retrieval statement that gives the full date you located the information and correctly names the database is required. (If you include an item or accession number, place it in parentheses after the title of your document.) Add the electronic address as a convenience to your reader when the database is complicated by the provider's size or complexity or when you retrieve a version of a document available only at that file address. The models here illustrate database citations from a CD-ROM and two online resources.

### 23. AGGREGATED DATABASE

Krauthammer, C. (1991, December 30). Why is America in a blue funk? *Time*, *138*, 83. Retrieved from UMIACH database. (Periodical Abstracts, Item: 1126.00 CD-ROM).

Freud, S. (1913). *Interpretation of dreams* (A. A. Brill, Trans.). New York: Macmillan. Retrieved March 1, 2002, from Classics in the History of Psychology database.

A title or author keyword search will lead to the document in the database. If the database were accessed on CD-ROM or a library server, the citation would be the same.

Bar-Tal, Y., Kishon-Rabin, L., & Tabak, N. (in press). The effect of need and ability to achieve cognitive structuring. *Journal of Personality and Social Psychology*. Abstract retrieved March 7, 2002, from Purdue University, Social Cognition Paper Archive and Information Center database: http//:www/psych.purdue.edu/~esmith/bt.html

This model provides information to retrieve this specific document from a database within a university site. (The identifier *Abstract* is added because it is not a full-text document.) Use this model for a specific article, data summary, or other specific document; it is also the model used for material obtained from an outline database.

### 24. COMPUTER SOFTWARE

HyperCard (Version 2.2) [Computer software]. (1993).
Cupertino, CA: Apple Computer.

Commonly available software is cited in the text. Only un-common software products require a References page entry like the one modeled here. Provide the version number, if available, in parentheses following the program or soft-ware name. Add the descriptive term *Computer software* in brackets followed by a period. Do not italicize names of computer programs.

## 61e.  Documenting other sources

### 25. MOTION PICTURES, AUDIO RECORDINGS, AND OTHER NONPRINT MEDIA

Curtiz, M. (Director). (1942). *Casablanca* [Motion
picture]. United States: Warner Bros.

Alphabetize a motion picture listing by the name of the person or persons with primary responsibility for the prod-uct. Identify the medium in brackets following the title, and indicate both country location and name of the distributor (as publisher). Other identifying information (director, scriptwriter, etc.) appears in parentheses as shown here.

### 26. INTERVIEWS AND OTHER FIELD SOURCES

These are identified in the text in parentheses (name, place, date) but are not listed on the References page. (See model 21.)

## 62  Sample References Page in APA Style

Authors are listed alphabetically.

Initials are used for first and middle names.

Do not use p. or pp. to indicate pages in a journal or magazine.

Date follows author (or title, if no author is identified).

Indent 5–7 spaces.

Use p. or pp. with page numbers in books or newspapers.

---

↕ 1"     ↕ 1/2"

Green Is     10

References

Allen, F. E. (1991, March 10). Great Lakes

cleanup enlists big volunteers. *The Wall*

*Street Journal*, p. B1.

Carlson, L., Grove, S. J., & Kangun, N. (1993).

A content analysis of environmental

advertising claims: A matrix methods approach.

*Journal of Advertising, 22*(9), 27–39.

Decker, C., & Stammer, L. (1989, March 4).

Bush asks ban on CFC to save ozone. *Los*

*Angeles Times*, p. A1.

Do people allow themselves to be that gullible?

(1994, September). *Earth First! 9*, 6.

Don't you wish we could just do this to CFC's?

(1994, December 7). [Natural gas advertisement.]

*Audubon, 12*, 7.

The Ecology Channel. (2004). Retrieved November

12, 2004, from http://www.ecology.com

Fogel, B. (1985). *Energy: Choices for the*

*future*. New York: Franklin Watts.

From this day onward I will restore the earth

where I am. (1994, December 7).

[Chevrolet advertisement.] *Audubon, 12*, 18–19.

Kennedy, D., & Grumbly, T. P. (1988). Automotive

emissions research. In A. Watson, R. R.

Bates, & D. Kennedy (Eds.), *Air pollution,*

*the automobile, and public health*

(pp. 3–9). Cambridge, MA: National Academy Press.

↕ 1"

Double-space throughout.

Only proper names and the first word in titles and subtitles are capitalized for books and articles.

Book and periodical titles are italicized.

---

*Sample References Page of a Student Essay in APA Format*

# *Chicago Manual* Style of Documentation

The most widely used documentation system in history, philosophy, religion, and the fine arts is that of *The Chicago Manual of Style,* 15th ed. (Chicago: University of Chicago Press, 2003). The *Chicago Manual* (CM) style places numbers in the text that correspond to notes at either the bottom of the page (footnotes) or the end of the paper (endnotes). Because citations are signaled only by small raised numbers, CM style calls less attention to documentation than the parenthetical in-text systems of MLA and APA.

## 63 Guidelines for Formatting Manuscripts

The CM guidelines for preparing manuscripts do not reflect the wealth of visually interesting options in fonts, point sizes, visual insertions, and other features available on modern word processing programs. If your instructor requests strict CM format, follow the guidelines here. If your instructor encourages more creative formats, use good judgment in displaying the information in your text. The following guidelines describe the preparation of the main body of your paper.

### Paper and printing

Print all academic assignments on clean white $8\frac{1}{2}$-by-11-inch paper in a standard font (e.g., Times New Roman, Courier) and point size (11–12) using a good-quality printer.

### Margins and spacing

Allow margins of one inch all around. Justify the left margin only. Use the tab key to indent the first line of each paragraph.

For prose quotations of more than one paragraph (or two lines of poetry), use the indent key to indent the entire quotation. Do not use quotation marks with such passages.

Double-space everything in the paper, including headings, quoted material, notes, and Bibliography entries.

### Page numbers

Set page numbers to print in the upper right margin of all pages, one-half inch below the top of the paper; do not use the word *page* or the abbreviation *p.* with page numbers. It is optional to include your last name before each page number—a protection in case pages become separated from the manuscript. Count but do not number the title page, so the first page of text begins with number 2.

### Title page

Attach an unnumbered title page. Center the title fifteen lines from the top. Four spaces below the title, center the word *By;* two spaces below that, center your name, the course name, your instructor's name, and the date.

## First page of text

Center the title on the first page using conventional title
case punctuation (capitalizing key words only). If your instructor asks for strict CM style, avoid using italics, underlining, quotation marks, boldface, unusual fonts, or an
enlarged point size for the title. Double-space to the first
paragraph and continue double-spacing throughout.

## Punctuation

Use one space after commas, semicolons, colons, periods,
question marks, exclamation points, and between the periods in an ellipsis.

## Visual information

Number all tables (charts, graphs) and figures (drawings,
photographs) sequentially. Write a clear caption for each.
Submit each on a separate unnumbered page inserted in
your manuscript immediately following the point in the text
it illustrates. At that point in the text, insert a reference to
the table ("see table 1") or figure ("see fig. 2").

# 64   Guidelines for In-Text Citations

## 64a.  Acknowledging sources

In the main body of the paper, mark each quotation, paraphrase, and summary of source material by inserting a
raised (superscript) Arabic number immediately after the
sentence or clause. The superscript number follows all
punctuation except dashes. Numbers run consecutively
throughout the text.

> Frank Lloyd Wright's "prairie style" was
> characterized by the houses he built in and around
> Chicago "with low horizontal lines echoing the
> landscape."[1] Vincent Scully sees these suburban
> buildings as one of Wright's most important
> influences.[2]

For each superscript number, write a corresponding
note, either at the end of the paper (an endnote, on a

separate page titled *Notes*) or at the foot of the page on which the number appears (a footnote).

> 1. *The Concise Columbia Encyclopedia*, 3rd ed., s.v. "Wright, Frank Lloyd."
>
> 2. Vincent Scully, *Architecture: The Natural and the Manmade* (New York: St. Martin's Press, 1991), 340.

## 64b. Bibliography

A Bibliography is required at the end of a *Chicago*-style paper. It lists all of the works you consulted in writing the paper, whether or not actually cited in a footnote or endnote. When you use endnotes, the Bibliography follows. Guidelines for assembling the Bibliography are as follows:

- Center the word *Bibliography* at the top of the page.

- Type the first line of each entry flush with the left margin.

- List all authors or editors in alphabetical order, last names first.

- List the names of coauthors in normal order, first names first, separated by commas.

- If two or more authors share the same last name, alphabetize by first name.

- If two or more works are by the same author, alphabetize by the title of the work. After the first listing, use a three-em dash to indicate the author's name for each subsequent work.

- If neither author nor editor is listed, alphabetize by title.

- Use periods followed by one space to separate the author from the title from the publication data.

- Capitalize all important words in the title.

- Underline or italicize the titles of published books, periodicals, or films.

- Use quotation marks to indicate the titles of articles, chapters, poems, and stories within published books.

- The entries in the Bibliography appear the same as they do on the Notes page, except that they are in alphabetical, not numerical, order and the name of the first (or sole) author is inverted (see Chapter 65).

CM

# 65 Guidelines for Endnote/ Footnote Citation

**Endnotes** are typed as one double-spaced list at the end of the text. The endnote format is easy to deal with, and it allows you to add or delete notes and change numbering with less fuss than footnotes entail.

The endnotes follow the last page of text, starting on a new page numbered in sequence. The title *Notes* is centered without quotation marks, one inch from the top of the page. Double-space before the first entry, within entries, and between entries. List entries in the order of the note numbers in your paper. Indent the first line of each note.

**Footnotes** enable readers to find information at a glance. Footnotes are placed at the bottom of the page on which the superscript numbers referring to them appear, four lines of space below the last line of text on that page.

**Numbers** in footnotes are aligned with the entry, followed by a period and one space before the first word. Indent each note.

A **Bibliography** is normally required to provide readers with a convenient way of identifying an author's full set of sources (see 64b).

## 65a. Documenting books: First reference

### 1. BOOK BY ONE AUTHOR

1. Lewis Thomas, *Lives of a Cell: Notes of a Biology Watcher* (New York: Viking, 1974), 76.

### 2. BOOK BY TWO OR MORE AUTHORS

2. Toby Fulwiler and Alan R. Hayakawa, *The Blair Handbook* (Boston: Blair, 2000), 234.

### 3. REVISED EDITION OF A BOOK

3. S. I. Hayakawa, *Language in Thought and Action*, 4th ed. (New York: Harcourt, Brace, 1978), 77.

### 4. EDITED BOOK AND ONE VOLUME OF A MULTIVOLUME BOOK

4. Tom Waldrep, ed., *Writers on Writing*, vol. 2 (New York: Random House, 1988), 123.

### 5. TRANSLATED BOOK

5. Albert Camus, *The Stranger*, trans. Stuart Gilbert (New York: Random House, 1946), 12.

### 6. REPRINTED BOOK

6. Zora Neale Hurston, *Their Eyes Were Watching God* (1937; reprint, New York: HarperPerennial, 1990), 32.

### 7. WORK IN AN ANTHOLOGY OR EDITED COLLECTION

7. John Donne, "The Good-Morrow," in *The Metaphysical Poets*, ed. Helen Gardner (Baltimore: Penguin, 1957), 58.

### 8. ARTICLE IN A REFERENCE BOOK

8. *The Concise Columbia Encyclopedia*, 3rd ed., s.v. "Behn, Aphra."

An alphabetically arranged book requires no page numbers. Begin with the author of the entry, if known.

### 9. ANONYMOUS BOOK

9. *The World Almanac and Book of Facts* (New York: World Almanac, 1995).

## 65b. Documenting periodicals: First reference

### 10. ARTICLE, STORY, OR POEM IN A MONTHLY OR BIMONTHLY MAGAZINE

10. Robert A. Linn and Stephen B. Dunbar, "The Nation's Report Card Goes Home," *Phi Delta Kappan*, October 1990, 127–43.

### 11. ARTICLE, STORY, OR POEM IN A WEEKLY MAGAZINE

11. John Updike, "His Mother Inside Him," *New Yorker*, April 20, 1992, 34–36.

### 12. ARTICLE IN A DAILY NEWSPAPER

12. Jane E. Brody, "Doctors Get Poor Marks for Nutrition Knowledge," *New York Times*, February 10, 1992, national edition, B7.

### 13. ARTICLE IN A JOURNAL PAGINATED BY VOLUME

13. Joseph Harris, "The Other Reader," *Journal of Advanced Composition*, 12 (1992): 34–36.

**CM**

### 14. ARTICLE IN A JOURNAL PAGINATED BY ISSUE

14. Helen Tiffin, "Post-Colonialism, Post-Modernism, and the Rehabilitation of Post-Colonial History," *Journal of Commonwealth Literature,* 23, no. 1 (1988): 189–95.

### 15. REVIEW

15. Mimi Kramer, "Victims." Review of *'Tis Pity She's a Whore,* New York Shakespeare Festival, *New Yorker,* April 20, 1992, 78–79.

## 65c. Documenting electronic sources

To document material consulted at a site on the World Wide Web, provide the following information:

- Author's name
- Title of document in quotation marks
- Title of complete work (if relevant) in italics
- Date of publication
- URL (address)

Date of access may be added in parentheses at the end of the entry but is not required.

### 16. PUBLISHED WEB SITE

16. Jonathon L. Beller, "What's Inside *The Insider?" Pop Matters Film,* 1999, http://popmatters.com/film/insider.html (accessed May 21, 2000).

### 17. PERSONAL WEB SITE

17. Toby Fulwiler, "Home page," Apr. 2, 2004, http://www.uvm.edu/~tfulwile (accessed May 6, 2004).

### 18. PROFESSIONAL WEB SITE

18. *Yellow Wallpaper Site,* University of Texas, 1995, http://www.cwrl.utexas.edu/~daniel/amlit/wallpaper/html (accessed December 12, 1999).

### 19. PUBLICATION REPRINTED ON THE WEB

19. Betsy Erkkila, "The Emily Dickinson Wars," *Emily Dickinson Journal* 5, no. 2 (1996),

http://www.colorado.edu/EDIS/Journal (accessed
June 2, 2002).

### 20. ARTICLE IN A REFERENCE DATABASE

20. *Encyclopaedia Britannica Online,*
s.v. "Victorian," http://www.britannica.com
(accessed May 3, 1999).

### 21. E-MAIL MESSAGE

21. Provide relevant information in the text.

### 22. PERSONAL INTERVIEW OR UNPUBLISHED LETTER

22. Provide relevant information in the text.

## 65e.  Documenting subsequent references to the same work

The second and any subsequent times you refer to a source,
include the author's last name followed by a comma, a
shortened version of the title, a comma, and the page
number(s).

23. Thomas, *Lives,* 99.

CM

## 66   Sample Endnote/Footnote Pages in CM Style

Owsley 2

|1"

recorded "in exultant tones the universal neglect that had overtaken pagan learning."[2] It would be some time, however, before Christian education would replace classical training, and by the fourth century, a lack of interest in learning and culture among the elite of Roman society was apparent. Attempting to check the demise of education, the later emperors established municipal schools, and universities of rhetoric and law were also established in major cities throughout the Empire.[3]

*Superscript numbers indicate source references.*

**CM**

|1"

Owsley 12

### Notes

*Individual note entries are double-spaced throughout.*

*Separate page(s) at end of paper include all references in numerical order.*

1. Rosamond McKitterick, *The Carolingians and the Written Word* (Cambridge: Cambridge University Press, 1983), 61.

*First line indents.*

2. J. Bass Mullinger, *The Schools of Charles the Great* (New York: Stechert, 1911), 10.

3. James W. Thompson, *The Literacy of the Laity in the Middle Ages* (New York: Franklin, 1963), 17.

4. O. M. Dalton, introduction, *The Letters of Sidonius* (Oxford: Clarendon, 1915), cxiv.

*Subsequent reference to a work requires only author last name or names, shortened title, and page number.*

5. Pierre Riche, *Education and Culture in the Barbarian West* (Columbia: University of South Carolina Press, 1976), 4.

6. Thompson, *Literacy of the Laity*, ———

*Sample Pages of a Student Essay with Endnotes in CM Style*

Kelly 5

The Teatro Olimpico was completed in 1564, the statues, inscriptions, and bas-reliefs for the *fronsscena* being the last details completed. Meanwhile, careful plans were made for an inaugural, which was to be a production of *Oedipus* in a new translation.[10] Final decisions were made by the Academy in February 1585 for the seating of city officials, their wives, and others, with the ruling that "no masked men or women would be allowed in the theatre for the performance." [11] The organization of the audience space was "unique among Renaissance theaters, suggesting . . . its function as the theater of a 'club of equals,' rather than of a princely court."[12] The Academy is celebrated and related to Roman grandeur by the decoration over the monumental central opening, where its motto, 'Hoc Opus,' appears.[13] It is difficult to make out the entrances.

*Superscript numbers indicate reference.*

*Notes are numbered consecutively throughout the paper.*

— 10. J. Thomas Oosting, *Andrea Palladio's Teatro Olimpico* (Ann Arbor: University of Michigan Research Press, 1981), 118.

— 11. Ibid., 120.

12. Marvin Carlson, *Places of Performance; The Semiotics of Theater Architecture* (Ithaca, Cornell University Press, 1989), 5.

13. Simon Tidworth, *Theaters: An Architectural and Cultural History* (London: Praeger, 1973), 52.

*Number is repeated from the text and indented.*

*If a source is the same as the immediately preceding work, use Ibid. and the page number.*

*Double-space throughout.*

**CM**

*Sample Page of a Student Essay with Footnotes in CM Style*

# Writing for Work

Businesses value efficiency and accuracy, and business communications mirror those objectives. Both written and oral communication in the workplace should be brief and to the point, each conforming to standard conventions of American English as outlined throughout this handbook. In most situations, it is safest to be courteous, honest, objective, and to use a fairly formal tone.

Gauging the needs of an audience and anticipating their questions are especially important in all business communication. Ask yourself to whom the communication is being addressed. What information do they already have? What else do they need to know? Who else will read what you have written or hear what you have said?

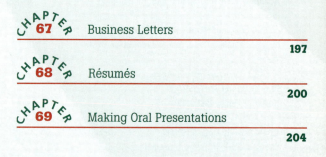

# 67 Business Letters

Business letters commonly request, inform, or complain, and they are often addressed to a reader unknown to the writer. State your purpose clearly, and provide all the information needed to make it easy for the reader to respond.

## 67a. Basic elements of business letters

### Paper

Business letters are typed on $8\frac{1}{2}$-by-11-inch paper, on one side only. Most use block format; that is, every element of the letter is typed flush with the left margin.

### Heading

Type the sender's address (but not name) and the date, single-spaced, approximately one inch from the top of the first page. Spell out street and town names and months in full. Abbreviate state names using standard postal abbreviations, followed by the ZIP code.

If you use letterhead stationery, type the date two line spaces below the letterhead address.

### Inside address

Type the recipient's address two line spaces below the heading. (If the letter is very short, add space here so that the letter will be centered on the page.) Include the person's full name (and title, if appropriate), followed by position or job title (if needed); name of the department or division within the company; company name; and full street, city, and state address.

When writing to an unknown person, always try to find out the name and its spelling, perhaps by calling the company switchboard. If you can find no name, use an appropriate title (Personnel Director or Claims Manager, for example) in place of a name.

### Greeting

Type the opening salutation two line spaces below the inside address (*Dear Dr. Schmertz, Dear Mei Ling Wong*), followed by a colon. If you and the recipient are on a first-name basis, you may use only the first name alone (*Dear Mei Ling*).

If you do not know the recipient's name, use *To Whom It May Concern* or some variation of *Dear Claims Manager*, or write *Attention: Marketing Director* (without a second colon). Avoid the old-fashioned *Dear Sir* or *Dear Sir or Madam*.

### Body

Begin the body of the letter two line spaces below the greeting. Single-space within paragraphs; double-space between paragraphs.

If your reason for writing is clear and simple, state it directly in the first paragraph. If it is absolutely necessary to detail a situation, provide background, or supply context, do so in the first paragraph or two; then move on to state your purpose in writing.

If your letter is more than a page long, type the addressee's last name, the date, and the page number flush with the right margin of each subsequent page.

### Closing

Type the complimentary closing two spaces after the last line of the body of the letter. The most common closings are *Sincerely, Cordially, Yours truly, Respectfully yours* (formal), and *Best regards* (informal). Capitalize only the first word of the closing, and follow the closing with a comma.

### Signature

Type your full name, including any title, four line spaces below the closing. Sign the letter with your full name (or just your first name if you have addressed the recipient by first name) in blue or black ink in the space above your typed name.

### Additional information

You may provide additional brief information below your signature, flush with the left margin. This may include recipients of copies of the letter (*cc: Jennifer Rodriguez*); the word *Enclosures* (or the abbreviation *enc.*) to indicate that you are also enclosing additional material mentioned in the letter; and, if the letter was typed by someone other than the writer, the writer's initials and the typist's initials (*TF/jwl*).

1"

405 Martin Street
Lexington, KY 40508      ] Heading
February 10, 2007

Barbara McGarry, Director
Kentucky Council on the Arts
953 Versailles Road      ] Inside address
Frankfort, KY 40602

Dear Ms. McGarry:      ] Greeting

John Huff, one of my professors at the University of
Kentucky, recommended that I write to you regarding
openings in the Council's internship program this
summer. I would like to apply for one of these positions
and have enclosed my résumé for your consideration.

As you will note, my academic background combines a
primary concentration in business administration with
1" ← a minor in the fine arts. My goal after graduation is a → 1"
career in arts administration, focusing on fundraising
and outreach for a major public institution.

I hope you'll agree that my experience, particularly my
work with the local Community Concerts association, is
strong preparation for an internship with the Council.
I would appreciate the opportunity to discuss my
qualifications with you in greater detail.

I will call your office within the next few weeks to see
about setting up an appointment to meet with you. In the
meantime, you can reach me at the above address or by
phone at (606) 555-4033.

Thank you for your attention.

Sincerely,
          ] Four line spaces for signature
Chris Aleandro

*Sample Business Cover Letter in Block Format*

## 67b.  Guidelines for business writing

Your reader's time, as well as your own, is valuable.

- Get to the main point quickly. Avoid unnecessary information and repetition.

- Write in simple, direct language. Keep your sentences straightforward and readable.

- Choose the active voice over the passive.

- Use technical terminology and jargon sparingly. Write out complete names of companies, products, and titles. Explain any unusual terms.

- Avoid emotional or offensive language and sexist constructions. Always be courteous, even when lodging a complaint.

- Use numbers or descriptive headings to help readers locate information quickly.

- Use graphs, charts, and other illustrations when they convey information more clearly than words.

# 68     Résumés

A résumé is a brief summary of an applicant's qualification for employment. It outlines education, work experience, and other activities and interests so that a prospective employer can decide quickly whether or not an applicant is a good prospect for a particular job. If the résumé is attractive to an employer, the potential employer will usually take two more steps: contacting your references and conducting a personal interview with you.

Try to tailor your résumé for the position you are seeking by emphasizing experience that is most relevant to the job. Preparing a résumé on a computer lets you revise it easily and quickly.

A résumé is usually sent out with a cover letter that introduces the applicant, indicates the position applied for, and offers additional information not conveyed on the résumé itself. Résumés should be brief and to the point, preferably no more than one page long (if relevant experience is extensive, more than one page may be acceptable). Résumé formats vary, but most include the following information.

# 68a. Basic elements of a résumé

## Personal information

Résumés begin with the applicant's name, address, and phone number, usually centered at the top.

## Objective

Many college résumés include a line summarizing the applicant's objective, naming either the specific job sought or describing a larger career goal.

## Education

Most first-time job applicants list their educational background first because their employment history may be limited. Name the last two or three schools attended (including dates of attendance and degrees), starting with the most recent. Indicate major areas of study. If your grade point average is high, list it; if you've received awards, list them—a résumé is not the place to be modest.

## Work experience

List all relevant jobs, most recent first, including company name, dates of employment, and a brief job description or list of duties. Use your judgment about listing jobs where you had difficulties with your employer.

## Special skills or interests

Mention special skills, interests, or activities that provide additional clues about your abilities.

## References

At the end of your résumé, you have a choice: Either include the line "References available on request" or provide the names, addresses, and phone numbers of two or three people—teachers, supervisors, employers—whom you trust to give a good reference for you. (Obtain their permission first.)

The advantage of the first method is that the employer must indicate an interest in you by contacting you about

# Chris Aleandro

**PRESENT ADDRESS**
405 Martin Street
Lexington, KY 40508
(606) 555-4033
caleandr@magic.uk.edu

**PERMANENT ADDRESS**
12 Rostow Road
Milwaukee, WI 53713
(414) 555-3421

**OBJECTIVE**
Internship in arts administration

**EDUCATION**
BA, University of Kentucky (expected May 2007)
Major: Business
Minor: Art History
Grade point average: 3.47

**AWARDS, HONORS**
Martin Perry Scholarship for Outstanding Business Major; Honors, School of Business

**EMPLOYMENT**

2005–2007
Habitat for Humanity: Cochaired campus fundraising drive that raised $55,000.

2004–2005
Community Concerts, Inc: Served as part-time promotion assistant, handling scheduling, publicity, subscription procedures, and fundraising.

2003–2004
Art in the Schools Program Volunteer, through the Education Division of the Lexington Center for the Arts: Trained to conduct art appreciation presentations in grade school classrooms, visiting one school a month.

2001–2003
Music City (part-time and summers): Worked as sales clerk and assistant manager.

**SPECIAL SKILLS**
Word, PowerPoint, Excel, Web page design

**REFERENCES**
Available on request

*Sample Traditional Résumé*

# Susan Anderson

**Current address**

222 Summit Street
Burlington, VT 05401

(802) 555-1234
susan.anderson@uvm.edu

**Telephone and e-mail**

**OBJECTIVE: Researcher/writer for nonprofit environmental organization.**

## EDUCATION

**University of Vermont,** School of Natural Resources, Geology and English double major. GPA: 3.6. Expected graduation, May 2007.

**Fairfield High School,** Fairfield, OH. 1999–2003. Activities included debate team, Spanish Club, student newspaper, field hockey, swimming.

## SKILLS

**Field research.** Extensive experience analyzing natural plant communities, quantifying data, surveying field sites, and drawing topographical site maps.

**Computer literacy.** Fluent in MS Word, Excel, PowerPoint, Adobe Premier, Sigmaplot, INFORM, QuarkXPress.

**Spanish.** Fluent after four years of secondary and college study, including AFS summer abroad in Quito, Ecuador.

## RELEVANT ENVIRONMENTAL COURSEWORK

Field Ecology Methods
Fundamentals of Field Science
Landscape Inventory and Assessment
Nature Writing

## RESEARCH EXPERIENCE

**Southwest Earth Studies**, June–August 2006. Internship to research acid mine drainage in the San Juan Mountains, CO; grant, National Science Foundation.

**Field Research of the Newark Rift Basin,** June 2005. Internship to study water flow in Newark, NJ, rift basin; Newark Environment Foundation Fellowship.

## COMMUNICATIONS EXPERIENCE

**Editorial Assistant,** *Wild Gulf Journal,* Chewonki Foundation, January 2005–December 2006. Edited 70-page quarterly journal of environmental education resources for the Lake Champlain watershed.

**Tutor,** Writing Center, University of Vermont, September 2004–December 2005. Counseled students on papers for introductory geology courses.

## LEADERSHIP EXPERIENCE

**English Majors' Student Representative,** University of Vermont, September 2004–May 2005. Elected to represent 200 English majors and participate as a voting member at faculty meetings and on curriculum revision committee.

**Local Foods Coordinator,** Onion River Coorperative, Burlington, VT, January 2004–May 2005. Ordered produce and coordinated pickups from local farms.

**REFERENCES:** Available on request

*Sample Skills-Based Résumé*

references, which lets you know where you stand. The advantage of the second is that employers have all the necessary information in one package to make a decision about interviewing you.

Write the cover letter to your résumé as a business letter, pointing out features of your attached résumé of special interest or elaborating on experience and interest for which there is no room on the résumé proper.

## 68b.  Types of résumés

In addition to the traditional résumé described in 68a, you can compose a skills-based résumé that includes essentially the same information as a traditional résumé except that it emphasizes what you can do as opposed to what you have done. (See pages 202–03 for samples of both types of résumés.)

# 69   Making Oral Presentations

Public speaking may be required in both classroom and work settings. In speaking, as in writing, it's important to present ideas with confidence, clarity, accuracy, and grace. In the professions, in business, and in government, good writers and speakers get listened to, promoted, and rewarded; poor ones do not. Approach the making of a public talk as you would a writing task, in stages. Allow time to analyze purpose, scope, and audience; time to research, organize, and add visual aids; and time to rehearse timing and delivery.

## 69a.  Interpreting the assignment

- **Know your purpose.** Are you presenting information, raising questions, arguing a position, or doing something else? You are persuasive to the degree you believe in and understand your topic, so select it with care.

- **Know your audience.** What you say and how you say it depend on whom you are talking to. Use your time to teach your audience something it doesn't already know, not to cover material already covered in your class or textbook. Tie new material to the theme of the class.

■ **Collaborate.** If collaboration is called for, follow these guidelines: (1) Don't proceed until all of you know what is expected. (2) Divide tasks according to ability. (3) Do your own part promptly, and hold others accountable for doing theirs. (4) Meet outside class so that your material is ready on time. (5) Plan in advance who will report what and for how long.

## 69b.  Preparing a speech

Texts meant to be spoken need to be simple, clear, and direct. Follow the same process as in writing a paper: *Plan, draft, research, revise,* and *edit* the material until you know and trust it. The following ideas detail such a process.

■ **Plan.** Allow time to explore a topic before committing to it. Don't try to prepare your whole oral report the night before it is due.

■ **Draft.** Write a full draft of your talk even if you don't intend to read it. Once drafted, it's easy to make an outline or notes from it from which to speak.

■ **Research.** Investigate reliable external sources so that you have fresh and detailed information to convey. Cite texts, quote experts, report survey results, and explain and illustrate on-site visits.

■ **Outline.** Speaking is preferable to reading most of the time. The "final draft" of an oral report is not a polished, proofread paper but rather a "speaking outline" or set of notes to be glanced at as needed. (If your report is more than a few minutes long and complex or includes quotations and statistics, index cards are more helpful in leading you through your talk.)

■ **Repeat deliberately.** Here's the time-tested advice for making speeches: *"Tell 'em what you're gonna tell 'em. Tell 'em. Then tell 'em what you've told 'em."* In written texts, repetition leads to boredom; in oral presentations, it increases understanding and memory.

■ **Create listening signposts.** Include word signposts to help your audience follow you. For example, tell your audience you are going to make three points; then

enumerate each accordingly: "The first point is . . . ,"
"The second point is . . . ," and so on.

- **Start strong.** Your opening sets the tone and
  expectations for what is to follow: To begin, ask
  provocative questions or tell brief stories. Make sure,
  by the end of your talk, that you have answered your
  questions or that the stories were pertinent to your
  topic.

- **Finish strong.** Many speakers map out their conclusion first and then work backward to make sure
  the text leads them there. With only five, ten, or fifteen
  minutes, be sure that when time is up, you've made
  the point you intended.

- **Simplify.** Prefer simple, jargon-free language, and
  repeat key words and phrases to reinforce your
  listeners' memory.

- **Prepare a text to be read.** Triple-space reading copy,
  use a large font size, leave wide margins to pencil in
  notes, and start new paragraphs on new pages. Plan
  on a minute per page to read wide-margined, triple-
  spaced text.

## 69c.  Standing up front

To give a speech means leaving your comfortable seat and
standing up front and center to gain attention. Remember,
even famous actors and speakers feel anxiety before speaking in front of live audiences. The following suggestions
may help alleviate nervousness.

- **Rehearse.** Deliver your oral presentation in the privacy
  of your room to check your understanding, pace, and
  timing. Rehearsing in front of a mirror or using a tape
  recorder may help you see and hear your presentation
  from the perspective of a listener.

- **Make the room your own.** If possible, set up the room
  to make you comfortable. If that means rearranging
  desks, tables, screens, or lecterns, do so. If you prefer
  your audience in a semicircle or in groups instead of
  straight rows, ask them to sit that way. Taking control
  of your space gives you ownership of your time in front
  of the class.

- **Maintain eye contact with friendly audience
  members.** While it's important to look around at the

whole audience, return periodically to the faces most receptive to your words—to smiles or nods or friends who will boost your confidence and keep you going smoothly.

## 69d. Selecting creative options

Depending on your task and time, you may want to enhance your presentation with certain materials or activities.

### PowerPoint Presentations

The PowerPoint computer program creates slides containing text, graphics, and photos for oral presentations. The slides can be printed on transparencies for an overhead projector or projected via a special computer monitor. The following tips will help you make a professional presentation.

- **Check the room in advance.** Make sure that the room can be dimmed and that the screen isn't facing the light. Check sight lines to be sure that the whole audience can see.
- **Estimate the distance** from the farthest seat to the screen. Use the sign painter's rule of thumb: one-inch letters can be read from ten feet, two-inch letters from twenty feet, and so on. Adjust type sizes accordingly.
- **Consider readability.** Complementary colors (red on green) may be hard to see, and other combinations (black on yellow) may need to be toned down. Choose light colors for backgrounds.
- **Make your organization visible.** If your outline has three main sections, show the main points in each, using one or more slides.
- **Use art carefully.** If a photo or graphic is the best way to convey information, use it; however, most clip art cartoon figures convey little information and look amateurish.
- **Pass out a printed handout** for important information you want your audience to carry away from your presentation.
- **Rehearse** with a computer and a tape recorder so that you can watch and listen to your presentation at the same time.

- **Use handouts.** Augment your talk by handing out relevant outlines, poems, stories, ads, articles, and illustrations.

- **Use prepared audiovisual aids.** Any of the following visual aids will increase attention as you speak: videos, films, tape recordings, maps, charts, sketches, photographs, posters, computer graphics, or transparencies shown on overhead projectors. Computer programs such as PowerPoint allow you to prepare professional-quality visual aids (see the box on page 207).

- **Be an audiovisual aid.** For some topics, a live demonstration may be appropriate. Even if you do not demonstrate a process, use body language to your advantage. Natural gestures help you maintain audience interest and reinforce what you are saying.

- **Ask your audience to write.** To engage an audience quickly and relax yourself at the same time, ask people to write briefly about some aspect of your topic before you speak. After a few minutes, ask them to talk about their ideas with a neighbor for several more minutes. Writing for even five minutes pulls people into your topic by causing them to think personally about it. To resume control, ask for several volunteer opinions, and use these as a bridge to your own presentation.

## Glossary of Usage

This glossary provides information about frequently confused, misused, and nonstandard words. It also lists colloquial usages that are common in informal writing but often unacceptable in academic writing.

**a, an**   Use *a* before words that begin with a consonant sound (*a* boy, *a* history), even if the first letter of the word is a vowel (*a* useful lesson). Use *an* before words that begin with a vowel sound (*an* antelope, *an* hour).

**accept, except**   *Accept* is a verb meaning "to receive" or "to approve" (*I* accept *your offer*). *Except* is usually a preposition meaning "excluding" (*He liked to eat everything* except *vegetables*).

**adapt, adopt**   *Adapt* means "to adjust" or "to accommodate"; it is usually followed by *to* (*It is sometimes hard to* adapt *to college life*). *Adopt* means "to take and use as one's own" (*My parents are* adopting *another child*).

**advice, advise**   *Advice* is a noun; *advise* is a verb (*I* advise *you to take my* advice *and study hard*).

**affect, effect**   *Affect* as a verb means "to influence" or "to produce an effect" (*That movie* affected *me deeply*). *Effect* is commonly used as a noun meaning "result" (*That movie had a profound* effect *on me*). *Effect* can also be a verb meaning "to bring about" (*Dr. Jones* effected *important changes as president*).

**all ready, already**   *All ready* means "fully prepared" (*The children were* all ready *for bed*). *Already* means "previously" (*The children were* already *in bed when I arrived*).

**all right, alright**   *All right* is always written as two words. *Alright* is nonstandard.

**all together, altogether**   *All together* means "all gathered in one place" (*The animals were all together in the ark*). *Altogether* means "thoroughly" or "completely" (*The ark was altogether too full of animals*).

**allusion, illusion**   *Allusion* means "an indirect reference" (*The movie had many allusions to Shakespeare*). An *illusion* is a misconception or false impression. (*Mr. Hodges created an optical illusion with two lines*).

**a lot**   *A lot* should always be written as two words.

**among, between**   Use *among* with three or more individuals, *between* with two. (*It was difficult to choose among all the exotic plants. There were significant differences between the two candidates*).

**amount, number**   Use *amount* with quantities that cannot be counted; use *number* with those that can. (*It took a great amount of paint to fix up the farmhouse. A large number of volunteers showed up to clean out the building*).

**and/or**   Avoid *and/or* except in technical or legal documents.

**anxious, eager**   *Anxious* is an adjective meaning "worried" or "uneasy." Do not confuse it with *eager*, which means "enthusiastic." (*Lynn is anxious about surgery.*)

**anyone, any one**   *Anyone* is a pronoun that refers to an unspecified person (*Anyone on the hill could have seen our campfire*). *Any one* refers to a single member of a group (*Each child may select any one toy from the toy box*).

**as**   *As* may be used to mean "because" (*We did not go ice skating as the lake was no longer frozen*), but only if there is no ambiguity. (*We canceled the meeting because* [not *as*] *only two people showed up.*)

**as, as if, like**   Use *like* to compare items (*Ken, like his brother, prefers to sleep late*). Avoid using *like* as a conjunction linking two clauses. Use *as* or *as if* instead (*Anne talks as if* [not *like*] *she has read every book by Ernest Hemingway*).

**awful, awfully**    *Awful* is an adjective meaning "inspiring awe." Do not use it to mean "disagreeable" or "objectionable." The adverb *awfully* means "in an awe-inspiring way"; avoid using it in the colloquial sense of "very."

**awhile, a while**    The one-word form *awhile* is an adverb that can be used to modify a verb (*We rested awhile*). Only the two-word form *a while* can be the object of a preposition (*We rested for a while*).

**bad, badly**    *Bad* is an adjective, so it must modify a noun or follow a linking verb, such as *be, feel,* or *become* (*John felt bad about holding the picnic in bad weather*). *Badly* is an adverb, so it must modify a verb (*Pam played badly today*).

**beside, besides**    *Beside* is a preposition meaning "by the side of" or "next to" (*The book is beside the bed*). *Besides* can be used as a preposition meaning "other than" or "in addition to" (*No one besides Linda can build a good campfire*). *Besides* is also an adverb meaning "furthermore" or "in addition" (*The weather is bad for hiking; besides, I have a cold*).

**between**    See *among, between.*

**bring, take**    The verb *bring* describes movement from a distant place to a nearer place; the verb *take* describes movement away from a place (*Dr. Gavin asked us to bring our rough sketches to class; she said we may take them home after class*).

**can, may**    *Can* is used to indicate ability, and *may* indicates permission (*I can see much better with my new glasses. May I borrow your dictionary?*).

**capital, capitol**    *Capital* refers to a city, *capitol* to a building where lawmakers meet (*Albany is the capital of New York. The civics class toured the state capitol last week*). *Capital* also means "accumulated wealth."

**cite, site**    *Cite* means "to quote for purposes of example, authority, or proof" (*Tracy cites several legal* *experts in her paper*). *Site* means "place or scene" (*Today we poured the foundation on the <u>site</u> of our future home*). Locations on the Internet are referred to as *sites.*

**complement, compliment**     *Complement* is a verb meaning "to fill out or complete" or a noun meaning "something that completes or fits with" (*The bouquet of spring flowers <u>complemented</u> the table setting*). *Compliment* is a verb meaning "to express esteem or admiration" or a noun meaning "an expression of esteem or admiration" (*Russ <u>complimented</u> Nancy on her choice of flowers*). As a noun, *compliment* means a flattering remark or action (*The team voted her captain, which she took as a <u>compliment</u>*).

**conscience, conscious**     *Conscience* is a noun referring to a sense of right and wrong (*His <u>conscience</u> would not allow him to lie*). *Conscious* is an adjective meaning "marked by thought or will" or "acting with critical awareness" (*He made a <u>conscious</u> decision to be more honest*).

**continual, continuous**     *Continual* means "occurring repeatedly" (*Liz saw a doctor about her <u>continual</u> headaches*). *Continuous* means "uninterrupted in space, time, or sequence" (*Eventually we grew used to the <u>continuous</u> noise*).

**council, counsel**     *Council* is a noun meaning "a group meeting for advice, discussion, or government" (*The tribal <u>council</u> voted in favor of the new land rights law*). *Counsel* is a noun meaning "advice" or "a plan of action or behavior" (*The priest gave <u>counsel</u> to the young men considering the priesthood*). It can also refer to a legal representative. As a verb, *counsel* means "to advise."

**criteria**     *Criteria* is the plural of *criterion,* which means "a standard on which a judgment is based" (*Many <u>criteria</u> are used in selecting a president, but a candidate's hair color is not an appropriate <u>criterion</u>*).

**data**     *Data* is the plural of *datum,* which means "an observed fact." But *data* is increasingly being used as a singular noun (*The data indicate* [or *indicates*] *that a low-fat diet may increase life expectancy*). The singular *datum* is rarely used.

**different from, different than**   *Different from* is preferred to *different than* (*Hal's taste in music is different from his wife's*). But *different than* may be used to avoid awkward constructions (*Hal's taste in music is different than* [instead of *different from what*] *it was five years ago*).

**disinterested, uninterested**   *Disinterested* means "unbiased" (*It will be difficult to find twelve disinterested jurors for such a highly publicized case*). *Uninterested* means "indifferent" or "unconcerned" (*Most people were uninterested in the case until the police discovered surprising new evidence*).

**enthused, enthusiastic**   As an adjective, *enthusiastic* is preferred (*Barbara is enthusiastic* [not *enthused*] *about her music lessons*).

**etc.**   Avoid ending a list with *etc.;* indicate that you are leaving items out of a list with *and so on* or *and so forth.*

**everyone, every one**   *Everyone* refers to an unspecified person (*Everybody wins in this game*). *Every one* refers to each individual member of a group (*Every one of these toys must be picked up*).

**except**   See *accept, except.*

**farther, further**   Use *farther* to refer to physical distances (*Boston is farther than I thought*) and *further* to refer to quantity, time, or degree (*We made further progress on our research project*).

**fewer, less**   *Fewer* refers to people or items that can be counted; *less* refers to general amounts. (*Fewer people went to the conference this year. We needed less space.*)

**firstly, secondly, thirdly**   These expressions are awkward; use *first, second,* and *third.*

**good, well**   *Good* is an adjective; it should not be used in place of the adverb *well* in formal writing

(*Mario is a good tennis player; he played well* [not *good*] *today*).

**hardly, scarcely**    Avoid phrases like *can't scarcely* and *not hardly* in formal writing; these are double negatives (*I can scarcely* [not *can't scarcely*] *keep my eyes open*).

**he or she, his or her**    Use *he or she* and *his or her* to avoid sexist language. For more on avoiding sexist language, see 24c.

**hopefully**    *Hopefully* is an adverb meaning "in a hopeful manner" (*The child looked hopefully out the window for her mother*). In formal writing, do not use *hopefully* to mean "I hope that" or "It is hoped that" (*I hope that* [not *Hopefully*] *Bob will remember his camera*).

**illusion**    See *allusion, illusion.*

**imply, infer**    *Imply* means "to express indirectly" or "to suggest"; *infer* means "to conclude" (*Helen implied that she had time to visit with us, but we inferred from all the work on her desk that she was really too busy*). A speaker implies; a listener infers.

**irregardless, regardless**    Do not use the nonstandard *irregardless* in place of *regardless* (*We will have the party regardless* [not *irregardless*] *of the weather*).

**its, it's**    *Its* is a possessive pronoun; *it's* is a contraction for *it is* (*It's hard to tear a baby animal away from its mother*).

**kind of, sort of**    Avoid using the colloquial expressions *kind of* and *sort of* to mean "somewhat" or "rather" (*My paper is rather* [not *kind of*] *short; my research for it was somewhat* [not *sort of*] *rushed*).

**lay**    See *lie, lay.*

**lead, led**    As a verb, *lead* means "to go first" or "to direct"; as a noun, it means "front position" (*Jill took* the <u>lead</u> in organizing the files). *Led* is the past-tense and past-participle form of the verb *lead* (*He* <u>led</u> *me to the cave*).

**learn, teach**  *Learn* means "to gain knowledge or understanding"; *teach* means "to cause to know" or "to instruct" (*Tonight Jim will* <u>teach</u> [not *learn*] *us a new dance.*)

**leave, let**  *Leave* means "to depart"; it should not be used in place of *let,* which means "to allow" (*When you are ready to leave,* <u>let</u> [not *leave*] *me give you a ride*).

**less**  See *fewer, less.*

**lie, lay**  *Lie* is a verb meaning "to recline" or "to rest in a horizontal position." Its forms are *lie, lay, lain. Lay* is a transitive verb (followed by a direct object) meaning "to put or set down." Its forms are *lay, laid, laid.* (<u>Lay</u> *the blanket on this spot and* <u>lie</u> [not *lay*] *down.*)

**like**  See *as, as if, like.*

**loose, lose**  *Loose* is an adjective meaning "not securely attached." *Lose* is a verb that means "to misplace" or "to undergo defeat" (*Be careful not to* <u>lose</u> *that* <u>loose</u> *button on your jacket*).

**may**  See *can, may.*

**may be, maybe**  *May be* is a verb phrase (*Charles* <u>may be</u> *interested in a new job*); *maybe* is an adverb meaning "possibly" (<u>Maybe</u> *I will speak to him about it*).

**media**  *Media* is the plural of *medium* (*Some people feel that the* <u>media</u> *were responsible for the candidate's loss*).

**moral, morale**  *Moral* is the lesson of a story or experience (*The* <u>moral</u> *is to treat others as you wish to be treated*). *Morale* is the mental condition or mood of a person or group (*The improvement in the weather lifted the crew's* <u>morale</u>).

**most**  Avoid using *most* to mean "almost" (*Prizes were given to* <u>almost</u> [not *most*] *all the participants*).

**myself**    *Myself* is a reflexive or intensive pronoun. Reflexive: *I hurt myself*. Intensive: *I will do it myself*. Do not use *myself* in place of *I* or *me*: *She gave the food to Jill and me* [not *myself*].

**nowheres**    *Nowheres* is nonstandard for *nowhere*.

**number**    See *amount, number*.

**passed, past**    *Passed* is the past-tense form of the verb *pass* (*She passed here several hours ago*). *Past* may be an adjective or a noun referring to a time before the present (*She has forgotten many details about her past life*).

**perspective, prospective**    *Perspective* is a noun meaning "a view"; do not confuse it with the adjective *prospective,* meaning "potential" or "likely" (*Mr. Harris's perspective on the new school changed when he met his son's prospective teacher*).

**precede, proceed**    *Precede* means "to come before"; *proceed* means "to go forward" (*The bridal attendants preceded the bride into the church; when the music started, they proceeded down the aisle*).

**principal, principle**    *Principal* is a noun meaning "head of a school or organization" or "an amount of money." It is also an adjective meaning "most important." *Principle* is a noun meaning "a rule of action" or "a basic law" (*My high school principal suggested a trip to Gettysburg, but my principal reason for going was my interest in the Civil War. I also wanted to learn about the principles of the US Constitution*).

**quotation, quote**    *Quotation* is a noun, and *quote* is a verb. Avoid using *quote* as a noun (*Sue quoted Jefferson in her speech, hoping the quotation* [not *quote*] *would have a powerful effect on her audience*).

**real, really**    *Real* is an adjective; *really* is an adverb. Avoid using *real* as an adverb (*Tim was really* [not *real*] *interested in buying Lana's car*).

**reason why**    *Reason why* is redundant. (*The reason* [not *reason why*] *we canceled the dance is that no one bought tickets.*)

**respectfully, respectively**    *Respectfully* means "in a respectful manner" (*The children listened to their teacher respectfully*). *Respectively* means "in the order given" (*The sessions on Italian, French, and Spanish culture are now scheduled for Tuesday, Wednesday, and Thursday, respectively*).

**set, sit**    *Set* means "to put" or "to place"; *sit* means "to be seated" (*Mary set her packages on the kitchen table. I sat in the only chair in the waiting room*).

**since**    Do not use *since* to mean "because" when there is any chance of ambiguity: *Because* [not *since*] *she sold her bicycle, Lonnie has not been getting much exercise. Since* here could mean either "because" or "from the time that."

**sit**    See *set, sit.*

**site**    See *cite, site.*

**somebody, someone, something**    These singular indefinite pronouns take singular verbs (*Somebody calls every night at midnight and hangs up; I hope someone does something about this problem soon*).

**sure, surely**    Avoid using the adjective *sure* to mean "certainly"; use *surely* or *certainly* instead (*It is certainly* [or *surely*; not *sure*] *cold today*).

**take**    See *bring, take.*

**than, then**    *Than* is a conjunction used in comparisons (*Dan is older than Eve*). *Then* is an adverb indicating time (*First pick up the files and then deliver them to the company office*).

**that, which**    Many careful writers reserve *that* for restrictive clauses and *which* for nonrestrictive clauses. (See 34c.)

**their, there, they're**    *Their* is the possessive form of the pronoun *they* (*Did they leave their books here?*). *There* is an adverb meaning "in or at that place" (*No,* *they left their books <u>there</u>*). *They're* is a contraction of *they are* (*<u>They're</u> looking all over for their books*).

**then**    See *than, then*.

**to, too, two**    *To* is a preposition used to indicate movement or direction toward something (*Nancy is walking <u>to</u> the grocery store*). *Too* is an adverb meaning "also" (*Sam is walking <u>too</u>*). *Two* is a number (*The <u>two</u> of them are walking together*).

**toward, towards**    *Toward* is preferred, but both forms are acceptable.

**utilize**    The verb *utilize* means "to put to use." It often sounds pretentious; *use* is sufficient. (*We were able to <u>use</u>* [not *utilize*] *the hotel kitchen to prepare our meals*).

**wait for, wait on**    *Wait for* means "to await" or "to be ready for." *Wait on* means "to serve" (*You are too old to <u>wait for</u>* [not *on*] *your mother to <u>wait on</u> you*).

**way, ways**    Do not use *ways* in place of *way* when referring to long distances (*Los Angeles is a long <u>way</u>* [not *ways*] *from San Francisco*).

**well**    See *good, well*.

**where**    *Where* is nonstandard when used in place of *that* (*I read <u>that</u>* [not *where*] *several of the factories will be closed in June*).

**whether, weather**    *Whether* is a conjunction referring to a choice between alternatives; the noun *weather* refers to the state of the atmosphere (*Mike wondered <u>whether</u> the <u>weather</u> would clear up for the game*).

**which, who, that**    Use *which* to refer to places, things, or events; use *who* to refer to people. Use *that* to refer to things or, occasionally, to a group or class of people. (*The parade, <u>which</u> was rescheduled for Saturday, was a great success. The man <u>who</u> was grand marshal said it was the best parade <u>that</u> he could remember.*)

**while**    See *awhile/a while*.

**who, whom**   Use *who* for subjects and subject complements; use *whom* for objects and object complements (*Who* revealed the murderer's identity? *It's not* whom *you'd expect*). (See 29d.)

**who's, whose**   *Who's* is a contraction of *who is* (*Who's* coming for dinner tonight?). *Whose* is the possessive form of *who* (*Whose* hat is lying on the table?).

**your, you're**   *Your* is the possessive form of the pronoun *you* (*Your* table is ready); *you're* is a contraction of *you are* (*You're* leaving before the end of the show?).

## Glossary of Grammatical Terms

**Absolute phrase**    A word group that modifies (describes) an entire sentence or clause, consisting of a noun and a participle, together with any accompanying modifiers, objects, or complements: *The opposition conceding, the committee approved the resolution.*

**Active and passive voice**    In the active voice, the subject of the sentence does the action: *Mary caught the fly ball.* In the passive voice, the subject receives the action: *The fly ball was caught by Mary.* Sometimes the actor is not identified at all in the passive-voice sentence: *The fly ball was caught.*

**Adjective**    A word that modifies (describes) a noun, a pronoun, or a phrase or clause used as a noun. *The bird-watchers spotted scarlet tanagers* (modifies the noun *tanagers*). *They were beautiful* (modifies the pronoun *they*). *To see them would be delightful* (modifies the phrase *to see them*).

**Adjective clause**    A clause that modifies a noun or pronoun elsewhere in the sentence. An adjective clause usually begins with *who, whose,* or *that* (relative pronouns) or *when, where,* or *why* (relative adverbs) and directly follows the word it modifies: *The book that you reserved is now available* (modifies the noun *book*).

**Adverb**    A word that modifies a verb, an adjective, or another adverb; it can also modify a clause or an entire sentence. *His judgment was made hastily* (modifies the verb *was made*). *The feathers are quite beautiful* (modifies the adjective *beautiful*).

**Adverb clause**    A clause that modifies a verb, an adjective, or an adverb or an entire phrase or clause. An adverb clause tells when, where, why, or how or specifies a condition. It is introduced by subordinating conjunctions such as *although, because,* *when, than, as,* or *since: The fish ride the tide as far as it will carry them.*

**Agreement**    See Chapter 28 and 29b.

**Antecedent**    The word to which a pronoun refers: *The dog that barked came into the house.* The relative pronoun *that* refers to *dog.*

**Appositive phrase**    A phrase that appears directly after a noun or pronoun and renames or further identifies it: *Ralph Nader, a longtime consumer advocate, supports auto emission control.*

**Article**    The word *a, an,* or *the,* used to mark a noun.

**Case**    See 29c.

**Clause**    Any group of related words with a subject and a predicate (a verb). A clause that can stand alone as a complete sentence is called an *independent clause: The moon rose.* A clause that cannot stand by itself as a complete sentence is called a *dependent clause* and must be joined to an independent clause: *The fog lifted when the moon rose.*

**Complement**    See *subject complement, object complement.*

**Complex sentence**    A sentence with one independent clause and at least one dependent clause. In the following example, the dependent clause is underlined: *The students assemble outside when the bell rings.*

**Compound-complex sentence**    A sentence containing at least two independent clauses and at least one dependent clause. In the following example, the dependent clause is underlined: *The first motorcyclists to arrive never ordered anything to eat; they just sat quietly until their hands stopped shaking.*

**Compound sentence**    A sentence consisting of two or more independent clauses usually joined by a comma and a coordinating conjunction (*for, and, nor, but, or, yet, so*): *They grew tired of waiting, so they finally hailed a taxi.*

**Conjunction**    A word that joins two or more words, phrases, or clauses. The coordinating conjunctions— *for, and, nor, but, or, yet,* and *so*—imply that the elements linked are equal or similar in importance. *Bill __and__ I went shopping. The bus will take you to the market __or__ to the theater.*

**Coordinating conjunction**   A word used to join equal grammatical elements: *for, and, nor, but, or, yet, so.*

**Correlative conjunction**   A word pair that connects similar words, phrases, or clauses: *either . . . or, neither . . . nor, both . . . and, not only . . . but also, whether . . . or. __Neither__ Jack __nor__ his brother was home. She __not only__ sings __but also__ dances.*

**Demonstrative pronoun**   A pronoun such as *this, that, these,* and *those,* used to identify a specific person, place, or thing: *__This__ is the largest one we have.* A demonstrative pronoun changes form to show number: *This* and *that* are singular; *these* and *those* are plural.

**Dependent clause**   See *clause.*

**Direct object**   A word that receives the action of a transitive verb: *The company paid its __workers__ a day early.* The direct object *workers* and its modifiers receive the action of being *paid.* To find the direct object, ask a *who* or *what* question about the subject and verb: *Whom did the company pay?*

**Gerund**   A verb form ending in *-ing* used as a noun: *__Swimming__ is fun. Swimming* is the subject of the verb *is.*

**Gerund phrase**   A phrase built around a gerund (the *-ing* form of a verb). A gerund phrase functions as a noun, subject, subject complement, direct object, or the object of a preposition. In the following example, the gerund phrase functions as a subject: *__Studying these essays__ takes a lot of time.*

**Helping verb**   One of the following words used with a main verb to alter tense or mood: *be, am, is, are, was, were, being, been; has, have, had; do, does, did; can, will, shall, should, could, would, may, might, must.* A helping verb always comes before a main verb: *__will__ sing, __is__ singing, __had__ sung.* Also called an *auxiliary verb.*

**Indefinite pronoun**   A pronoun that does not refer to any specific person, animal, place, thing, or idea:

*anyone, everybody, something, many, few,* and *none. Many are called, but few are chosen.*

**Independent clause**    See *clause.*

**Indirect object**    A person or thing to whom (or for whom) the action of the verb is directed. An indirect object precedes a direct object and is a noun or a pronoun: *The boss gave us an assignment.* To find the indirect object, identify the verb and the direct object and ask, *To or for whom?* or *To or for what?* To whom did the boss give an assignment? He gave it to *us.* So *us* is the indirect object.

**Infinitive**    The word *to* followed by a verb: *to sing, to walk.*

**Infinitive phrase**    A phrase built around an infinitive that functions as a noun, adjective, or adverb. Noun: *To raise a family is a lofty goal.* Adjective: *He has the duty to protect his children.* Adverb: *My father worked to provide for his family.*

**Interjection**    A word that shows surprise, dismay, or strong emotion, often appearing in speech or dialogue and usually taking an exclamation point: *Ouch! That pipe is hot!*

**Interrogative pronoun**    A pronoun used to ask questions: *who, what,* or *whose. Who is there? Whose footsteps did I hear?*

**Intransitive verb**    See *transitive and intransitive verbs.*

**Irregular verb**    See *regular and irregular verbs* (see also 27b).

**Linking verb**    A verb that links two equivalent terms and functions as an equal sign: *be, become, seem,* and verbs describing sensations, including *appear, look, feel, taste, smell,* and *sound.* For example: *Sue is nice. Sue = nice.*

**Modifier**    A word, phrase, or clause that describes or qualifies the meaning of a word. Modifiers include adjectives, adverbs, prepositional phrases, participial phrases, some infinitive phrases, and adjective and adverb clauses.

**Mood**  The aspect of a verb that expresses the speaker's attitude toward or relation to the action. English verbs have three moods: (1) the *indicative* (facts, opinions, questions): *It is cold;* (2) the *imperative* (commands or directives): *Stop!* and (3) the *subjunctive* (wishes, requirements, or conditions contrary to fact): *If I were you, . . .*

**Noun**  A word that names a person, animal, place, thing, or idea: *woman, dog, canyon, vase, virtue.* A **proper noun** names particular people, animals, places, things, or ideas: *Marie Curie, Black Beauty, Kentucky, Porsche 911, Catholicism.* A **common noun** applies to any member of a class or group: *scientist, horse, state, ship, religion.* A **count noun** refers to one or more individual items that can readily be counted: *one book, two books.* A **noncount noun** refers to entities that cannot be counted individually—*water, oil.* (Although most nouns come in singular and plural forms, noncount nouns seldom have a plural.) A **collective noun** refers to groups—*crowd, couple, flock*—and may be singular or plural. A **possessive noun** indicates ownership and requires an apostrophe and an *s: a mother's* love.

**Noun clause**  A clause used as a subject, an object, or a subject complement. A noun clause usually begins with *who, what,* or *which* (relative pronouns) or with *how, when, where, whether,* or *why* (subordinating conjunctions). In the following example, a noun clause is the subject: *What I want is a good job.*

**Noun phrase**  A phrase containing a noun, a pronoun, or an infinitive and all its modifiers: *The famous and venerable institution is bankrupt.*

**Object**  See *direct object, indirect object.*

**Object complement**  A word or word group that renames or describes a direct object. It always comes after the direct object: *Tonight we will paint the town red.* The adjective *red* modifies the direct object *town.*

**Object of a preposition**  See *prepositional phrase.*

**Participial phrase**  A phrase built around a past participle (usually ending in *–ed* or *–d*) or the present participle (ending in *–ing*): *Striking a blow for free-dom, the Minutemen fired back.*

**Participle, past**    A verb form usually ending in *-d, -ed, -n, -en,* or *-t: guided, walked, chosen.* A past participle functions as a main verb (*walked*), often with a helping verb (*had walked*), but it may also be used as a modifier (*broken windows*).

**Participle, present**    A verb form ending in *–ing* that is usually used with a helping verb to form a main verb (*is going*) but can also be used as an adjective (*the going rate*).

**Parts of speech**    A system for classifying words according to their grammatical function: *Nouns, pronouns, verbs, adjectives, adverbs, prepositions, conjunctions,* and *interjections* are the parts of speech.

**Passive voice**    See *active and passive voice.*

**Personal pronoun**    A pronoun used to refer to a person or thing: *I, me, you, she, her, he, him, their, it.* For example: *I asked you to buy it for me.*

**Phrase**    A group of related words that lack a subject, a predicate, or both. Most phrases function as modifiers (adjectives, adverbs) or as subjects or objects (nouns). See *absolute phrase, appositive phrase, gerund phrase, infinitive phrase, noun phrase, participial phrase, prepositional phrase, verb phrase.*

**Possessive pronoun**    A pronoun used to show ownership: *my, mine, your, yours, her, hers, his, its, our, ours, your, yours, their, theirs.* For example: *I lent her my books.* (See Chapter 29.)

**Predicate**    The verb of a sentence, along with its objects and modifiers. Usually, the predicate is at the end of the sentence: *A woman in a yellow raincoat ran to catch the bus.*

**Preposition**    A word that connects a noun or pronoun to other words in the sentence. Common prepositions include *about, above, across, after, around, at, before, behind, below, beside, between, beyond, by, down, during, of, on, over, since, through, to, toward, under,* and *with.*

**Prepositional phrase**    A phrase consisting of a preposition, its object, and any related modifiers: *The new book was hailed with great fanfare.*

**Progressive verb forms**   See Chapter 27.

**Pronoun**   A word that substitutes for a noun. The word the pronoun replaces is called its *antecedent*. A pronoun must agree with its antecedent in terms of person, number, and gender. *Sean helped Alicia paint her room.* *Alicia* is the antecedent of the pronoun *her.* See also *demonstrative pronoun, indefinite pronoun, interrogative pronoun, personal pronoun, reflexive or intensive pronoun,* and *relative pronoun.*

**Reflexive or intensive pronoun**   A pronoun ending in *–self* or *–selves* that refers to the subject: *myself, yourself, themselves. Dave cut himself while shaving.* Called an *intensive pronoun* when it emphasizes or "intensifies" an antecedent: *I talked to the president herself.*

**Regular and irregular verbs**   A regular verb forms the past tense and the past participle by adding *–ed* or *–d* to the base: *talk, talked, talked.* An irregular verb follows no such rules: *sing, sang, sung; begin, began, begun;* and so on. (See Chapter 27.)

**Relative pronoun**   A pronoun such as *who, whom, whoever, which, whichever, that, what,* or *whatever* that introduces a dependent clause and "relates" that clause to an antecedent earlier in the sentence: *She chose the knife that cut best.*

**Sentence**   A word group consisting of at least one independent clause: a subject (noun or pronoun) and a predicate (verb). See also *complex sentence, compound-complex sentence, compound sentence,* and *simple sentence.*

**Simple sentence**   A sentence consisting of a single independent clause (subject and predicate) and no subordinate clause: *John ran. Monkeys eat bananas.*

**Subject**   A word or word group that names who or what performs the action of the sentence or tells who or what the sentence is about. The subject usually comes at the beginning of a sentence: *A woman in a yellow raincoat ran to catch the bus.* The **simple subject** of a sentence is the person or thing that performs the action of the predicate: *John ran.* A

**compound subject** includes two or more subjects linked by a coordinating conjunction: *Books, records, and videotapes* filled the room.

**Subject complement**   A word that renames or describes the subject of a sentence. It follows a *linking verb* (*be, become, seem,* or *appear;* see 27d). Whatever appears before the linking verb is the subject; whatever appears after it is the subject complement: *My mother's <u>uncle</u> is the factory <u>foreman</u>.*

**Subjunctive mood**   A mood used to express wishes, requests, recommendations, and conditions contrary to fact: *I would be happier if I <u>were</u> with you.* (See 27g.)

**Subordinating conjunction**   A word that introduces a dependent (subordinate) clause: *<u>After</u> we arrive, we will eat.*

**Transitive and intransitive verbs**   A transitive verb takes a direct object (receives the action): *Joey <u>grew</u> tomatoes last summer.* An intransitive verb does not take a direct object: *Sheila <u>slept</u>.* (See 27d.)

**Verb**   A verb describes an action (*The logger <u>fells</u> the tree*) or a state of being (*The air <u>is</u> fragrant*). The verb of a sentence changes form to show *person, number, tense, voice,* and *mood.* English also has many phrasal verbs (multiword verbs): *The rocket <u>went off</u> with a bang.* (See Chapter 27.)

**Verbal**   A verb form that does not change form to show person or number. There are three types of verbals: *infinitive,* the base form of the verb, usually preceded by the word *to* (*to visit*); *gerund,* the *-ing* form of the verb used as a noun (*visiting*); and *participle,* the past participle, usually ending in *-ed* or *-d* (*visited*), as well as the present participle ending in *-ing* (*visiting*). After prepositions and certain verbs, the *to* of an infinitive disappears: *She let them visit their cousins.*

**Verb phrase**   The main verb of a clause and its auxiliaries: *The college <u>has been having a difficult year</u>.*

# Index

**229**

Asides, within parentheses, 96

*as, as if, like,* 210–11

Assertion, opening for written piece, 29

Associations
in APA References, 177, 182
in MLA Works Cited, 153

Associative structure, 7

Asterisk (*), in Internet search, 121

Audience, 3–4
instructors as, 4
for oral presentations, 204–5, 208
use of technical terms, 42–43

Audio recordings
in APA References, 184
italics for name of, 110
in MLA Works Cited, 162–63

Audiovisual aids, oral presentations, 208

Authors
in APA in-text citations, 168–70
in APA References, 175–78
in CM bibliography, 190–91
in MLA in-text citations, 142–44
in MLA Works Cited, 150, 152–63

Automatic phrases, 34–35

Auxiliary verbs, 57–58
modal auxiliaries, 58

*awful, awfully,* 211

*awhile, a while,* 211

# B

*bad, badly,* 73–74, 211

Balance, in written piece, 5

Bartelby.com, 122

*BC* (before Christ), 114

*BCE* (before the Common Era), 114

*be*
as auxiliary verb, 57–58
as irregular verb, 54
as linking verb, 59
past tense forms, 63
past tense of, 64

present tense forms, 63
present tense of, 64
with strong verbs, 37

*become,* as linking verb, 59

*beside, besides,* 211

*between, among,* 210

Bias
of authors, 126–27
by field researcher, 130–31
in written piece, 7

Biblical citations, and colon, 90

Bibliography
APA References, 174–85
CM format, 189
MLA Works Cited, 149–63
purpose of, 190
working bibliography, 119

*Biographical Dictionary,* online, 122

.biz site, 127

*Black,* use of term, 45

Block format, quotations, 116, 132, 171

Body language, interview subjects, 124–25

Body of letter, business letters, 198

Book in series, in MLA Works Cited, 154

*Book Review Digest, The,* 126

Books
in APA References, 175–78
in CM endnotes/footnotes, 190–91
in MLA Works Cited, 152–55, 159

Boolean logic, 121

*both,* and pronoun-antecedent agreement, 69

Brackets, 99–100
to clarify meaning, 99, 133–34

*bring, take,* 211

Business letters, 197–200
colon in salutation, 90
cover letter of résumé, 200–201
example of, 199
parts of, 197–98
writing guidelines, 200

Business names, capitalizing, 106